Praise for *The Path of Life*

"Lisa Robertson is one of my dearest friends and has one of the most delightful and vivacious relationships with God. She has walked her various life paths with God in gracious, honest, insightful ways that have inspired me and helped me grow. If you're looking for a mentor to help you know how to face all that's ahead of you with a sense of peace and wisdom, this book should be your next read! I give *The Path of Life* my highest recommendation."

—Lysa TerKeurst, #1 *New York Times* bestselling author
and president of Proverbs 31 Ministries

"I am so pleased that Lisa Robertson has written this book based on Psalm 16. Lisa's love for Jesus Christ is an inspiration to many and she has much wisdom to offer anyone seeking to travel on The Path of Life."

—Nicky Gumbel, Vicar of Holy Trinity Brompton, England

"One of the most frequent questions that clergy hear is 'What does God want me to do?' With lucid prose and engaging personal stories, Lisa explains how the Scriptures answer that question. Recommended for clergy to share with their flock, *The Path of Life* will encourage, guide, and bless those who want to do God's will."

—The Reverend Andrew Buchanan, Senior Pastor,
Galilee Church, Virginia Beach, Virginia

"Lisa has known my family almost my entire life. Sometimes when you have an 'adventurous path' as a young man, especially one that can seemingly take you away from God's plans as I did, those memories can either hurt or help you. In my case, I remember my parents loving me throughout the entire journey. Lisa has profound wisdom for everybody, parents and nonparents alike, as we all endeavor to love people better through this journey called life. I highly recommend *The Path of Life*."

—Carl Lentz, Senior Pastor, Hillsong Church NYC

"The path of the Christian life is relatively simple, but our experience on it is not. Lisa helps bring clarity and wisdom to the twists and turns we all face on our journeys with the Lord."

—Katherine and Jay Wolf, cofounders of the nonprofit Hope Heals; coauthors of *Hope Heals*

"Our journey starts with a first breath and then the first step. We may take the high road, the low road, or the road less traveled. Robertson guides us via the Bible's GPS on this amazing path of life. Enjoy the journey, for the destination is eternal. Read *The Path of Life* and reap the fruits either side of the path."

—Nigel Mumford, international speaker, author, founder of By His Wounds, Inc., and Priest Associate for Healing, Galilee Church, Virginia Beach, Virginia

"No matter what path you find yourself on—whether it's filled with surprises, hardships, or joy—you'll find your touchpoint in this book. Drawing on more than forty years of marriage, parenting, and following Christ, Lisa Robertson curates a wealth of scriptural insight and real-life stories that point us toward the best path of all: *the path of life!*"

—Jodie Berndt, bestselling author of *Praying the Scriptures for Your Children*

The PaTH OF LIFE

The Path OF LIFE

Walking in the Loving Presence of God

Lisa Robertson

EMANATE
BOOKS

Published in Nashville, Tennessee, by Emanate Books, an imprint of Thomas Nelson. Emanate Books and Thomas Nelson are registered trademarks of HarperCollins Christian Publishing, Inc.

Thomas Nelson titles may be purchased in bulk for educational, business, fund-raising, or sales promotional use. For information, please e-mail SpecialMarkets@ThomasNelson.com.

The names of some of the individuals featured throughout this book have been changed to protect their privacy.

ISBN 978-0-7852-2359-7 (eBook)
ISBN 978-0-7852-2356-6 (TP)

Library of Congress Control Number: 2019933672

Printed in the United States of America
19 20 21 22 23   LSC   10 9 8 7 6 5 4 3 2 1

This book is dedicated to

Tim, who makes our path together such an
awesome adventure every day. The first time
we went to church together, I flipped open my
Bible and "happened" to read this verse:

Oh, magnify the LORD with me.
And let us exalt His name together.
(Psalm 34:3 NKJV)

I didn't know we would be married, but I was sure we
would always be friends. And I love that we are both.

Contents

Foreword

KORIE ROBERTSON

Before I tell you how incredible this book is going to be and how awesome Lisa is, can I tell you the story of how we met?

It was in the most unlikely of places: a limo on the way to the White House Correspondents' Dinner. I know that sounds a bit like a "humble brag" and I guess it kind of is, so please forgive me! It was 2014 and God had done immeasurably more than we could have asked or imagined with a little television show about our crazy Louisiana family. He had taken our meager offering of a prayer at the end of every episode and placed our show in millions of homes in America and more than one hundred countries around the world. And on this night, we were heading to dinner with the president! My mom's first comment when I told her we were going was, "Good thing I taught you table manners!"

We climbed into the limo and Lisa and her husband, Tim, were there, looking beautiful and dashing in a gown and tux. Willie's tux pants that I brought for him didn't fit, so he was wearing black jeans, a white shirt, a black jacket (without a tie; he claimed you couldn't see it anyway because of his beard) and his red, white, and blue bandana. I'm pretty sure he was the only one there in jeans and a bandana. I, at least, had on a gown, so hopefully they would let us in!

We knew of Tim and Lisa. They were the Robertsons—of the *700 Club* Robertsons! That's pretty much all we knew, but that in itself was a big deal. Their family has done incredible things for the kingdom of God through their television network and the many great works they do around the world; so we knew of them, and were excited to meet them.

Once in the limo, Willie and I argued on the way there whether or not we would actually get to meet the president and First Lady. I had envisioned it like a giant meet-and-greet line where everyone walked past, shook their hands, and maybe got a photo op. They all informed me that there would be three thousand plus attendees at this event . . . that wasn't going to happen. We all had a good laugh about my ignorance and were on our way.

As soon as we walked into the Washington Hilton, a secret service agent walked up to Willie and me, leaned in, and whispered, "Mr. and Mrs. Robertson, the president would like to meet you." We were whisked behind the curtains to a small room where President and Mrs. Obama were standing along with a few other people: Conan O'Brien (who was the host of the night), his beautiful wife, and Nicole Kidman were among them. Despite Willie wearing denim to a formal dinner, this night was turning out to be pure magic!

The president and First Lady couldn't have been more kind and gracious. They told us they watch our show on Air Force One and thanked us for the positive values we were portraying on television. As we walked away one of the president's aides gave Willie a box of presidential cufflinks. We walked back out to our table in a state of shock to find Tim and Lisa waiting to hear about our exciting little detour, and a lifelong friendship was born.

Have you ever heard the term *lagniappe*? It's a Louisiana-French word we use around here that means "something given as a bonus, or a special gift." It's like the piled-high icing on top of the cupcake, the gravy, the extra little bit of good stuff that you didn't know was coming, or if you knew it was coming, you didn't expect it to be that good.

Well, I've always said Lisa was my lagniappe from this special night. We got to meet a lot of famous people at the dinner, even shake hands with the president and First lady, but meeting Lisa was that bonus, that extra-special gift that God handed out to me that I didn't see coming.

On this night, we were on the "surprising path" that you'll read about later, but since meeting Lisa, I've walked down difficult paths, come across potholes, been on tough parenting paths that put me on my knees, and even questioned the path that God was taking me down. Over the last few years, Lisa's words and prayers at just the right time have taught me and encouraged me along my journey.

It would have been easy for her to write a book about the ways God has blessed her family, but this is simply not that book. The Word of God pours out of her because she has spent a lifetime seeking Him. She has chosen to walk in His ways, and has experienced all the paths she writes about. Yes, God has blessed their family, but as with most of us, Lisa's deep understanding of His truth comes from the difficult things He has brought her through.

I love how in life, and in her writing, Lisa doesn't shy away from the hard paths, disappointments, the time her family had to forgive the seemingly unforgivable, the moments she questioned if God is actually real, her own parenting fears, the struggles within the church, and the times of waiting on answers. I also loved reading of her triumphs, the times God gave clear answers to her prayers, the times she didn't waiver even though she couldn't see clearly God's plan, the way she has learned to pack gratefulness in her bag for all life's paths.

Don't you love it when you find that friend who simply walks in the path God has for her and cheers you on in yours? She has done that for me and will do that for you in these pages. I've had the great privilege to know her, laugh with her, and learn from her over the years. You'll get that privilege in the pages of this book. May it be the lagniappe your soul needs as you read and discover the path God has laid out for you and know more fully His goodness and grace in every step.

Introduction

I first noticed the "path of life" when a wedding gift was delivered to our house. A handwritten note contained this message: "Tim and Lisa, May God bless your marriage. Love, The Ditchfields, Psalm 16:11."

I have long forgotten what the gift was, but I have never forgotten the card. When I looked up the verse and read it, the words resonated in me, and they have become a truth that guides me.

> You will make known to me the path of life;
> In Your presence is fullness of joy;
> In Your right hand there are pleasures forever. (Psalm 16:11 NASB)

The first time I read this verse, I thought about the variety of ways God had guided my life. The questions lingered: *Is there a path that God has for me? Can I find it? Will I take it? What does this verse mean to me?*

After our wedding in Denver, we moved to Massachusetts, where we quickly encountered questions about where we would live, where we would work, and which church we would attend. Each of these decisions shaped our path. With each one, the questions remained the same. *Is this God's best path for us? Is this the next step?* Whether the decisions were easy or difficult, the words of Psalm 16:11 continually guided us.

There are three powerful promises in this one verse. First, God will make the path known. His path for me is not hidden or a secret. If I look for it, I know I will find it, simply because He promises to make it known to me. My path is always there. This is not complicated if I focus and pay attention to God's leading in my life.

Second, when I am in His presence, I will discover "fullness of joy." The promise is short, simple, and powerful: I will be filled with joy when I am in God's presence. Being joy-filled means that there is no room for other things, like worry, anger, fears, or frustrations. Fullness of joy comes with the confidence that God's love, plans, and presence fill my life. This does not say that I will find joy only if I look for it, behave myself, or earn it. Joy is there because God's presence is there.

The third promise is "pleasures forever" in His presence. What stands out here is the amazing generosity of God. Two words used in this verse—*fullness* and *forever*—give a sense of being complete. When something is full, there is no room for lack. Forever means forever. Not just a minute or a day, but forever! These promises hinge simply on my willingness to follow God's path for my life. He will show me the way and fill my life with His joy and eternal pleasure. I may have been young when I read these words, but I wasn't stupid. Seeking all that God has for me continues to be the goal of my life.

As I moved from one stage of life to the next, the theme of a "path of life" stood out to me as I read the Bible. The path of life is created by God just for you. As you already know, this path is not just "straight and narrow." God has a path for each one of us, and along our paths we are certain to experience a wide variety of different terrains. It won't take long before we discover some difficulties. There will be times when our paths will be full of surprises.

Surprises on the path might be filled with joys and challenges.

Many stories throughout Scripture illustrate the different kinds of surprises God has for His people.

Have you ever thought about how you might respond to a burning bush? Or what if you saw men in a fiery furnace walking with an angel? (Some believe it may have been Jesus in the furnace with the three Hebrew children.) Another surprise: Esther, a young Jewish orphan girl, becomes a queen? Jesus was full of surprises too: He turned water into wine and fed thousands with just a few loaves of bread and a couple of fish. And He topped it all off with His spectacular resurrection. Pay attention and look for the surprises He has for you!

Prayer is important for our travels along the path. Throughout the Bible, we meet people who pray the same prayers that we pray when we ask God for help, guidance, wisdom, patience, and forgiveness. Like the people of old, we need God's help on our journey too.

On my path, I continue to learn about myself and about the Lord through my years of being a parent. I am intrigued by the challenge of imitating the ways God parented me as I struggled to parent our children. God is patient, kind, loving, and He doesn't envy or boast (1 Corinthians 13:4).

Every one of us is familiar with the difficult path, but did you know the Bible states there is a "hard path that flows with abundance"? Even in times of difficulty, in the hard places, He blesses us with abundance—learning how to trust God, receiving His guidance, insight, and wisdom. Innovation and inspiration are also some of the benefits as we walk on the difficult path.

Like the seasons, the path will change too. Nothing lasts forever; all of us find ourselves on the path of change.

The path of joy is where we learn that we can experience God's fullness of joy no matter what our circumstances may be. It doesn't necessarily mean we will be happy, but God's fullness of joy is attainable simply because we are in His presence.

The narrow path is unique to each one of us, marked by individual challenges and callings; narrow paths can be hard and are often lonely.

Along the way, we may stumble over some potholes. Potholes are tormenting voices we hear in our heads that lie to us, condemn, and judge us. If we aren't careful, these potholes can derail our journey.

Other paths in the Bible include a path in the sky, a path in the sea, a path of the ancestors, and my favorite path: "the path that no one knew was there" (Psalm 77:19).

Finding God's path for your life is not a mystery or impossible. People have always been eager to find God's way, and the people of the Bible are no different. Their prayers specifically asked God to lead them, teach them, show them, and not let them be put to shame. We can pray the same prayers: lead me, teach me, protect me. God is so faithful to us, and He makes it clear that He will teach us, show us, speak to us, and guide us on our path. We don't need to worry because God is there, and He can show us the way.

From my experience, I never see the whole path—just one step. When I ask the Lord to show me the way or to help me make a wise decision, often I have this thought, *Do what you know to do.* Or simply, *Take the next step. Just one step.*

Most of the time, I know what that one step should be. It is usually a simple step. Make a phone call, write a note, or be patient. Don't say that to them. Or, *do* say that! When you prayerfully take the next step and risk to follow God, you will find yourself on God's path for your life.

Many times the path is obvious in light of God's Word. Psalm 119:35 says it this way: "Make me walk along the path of your commands, for that is where my happiness is found." God's path for us is anchored in His commands. Begin with the Great Commandment of Jesus: "Love the Lord your God with all of your heart, mind, soul, and strength and your neighbor as yourself" (Matthew 22:35–39). What a difference it would make if we lived each day with this command as our priority!

Following God's path is a very important part of our Christian walk. We must decide to follow the path of life, or we could find ourselves on paths the Bible describes as slippery, dark, or muddy. We do not want to be there.

Yes, there have been times when I have wandered off God's best path for me. To my relief, and with God as the guide, He is always there to show me exactly how to get back on the path of life.

The paths of the Bible have several things in common. A path always has a destination, often to water, food, or shelter. You are never the first one on a path. Someone has always gone ahead of you. Most paths have existed for a long time; they are not brand-new. God has called each one of us to walk the path He has prepared for us. As we travel on this journey, we will walk on different terrains: rocky, steep, windy, slippery, and more.

Isaiah 30:21 says, "Whether you turn to the right or to the left, your ears will hear a voice behind you, saying, 'This is the way; walk in it'" (NIV). God has prepared the path for you, He guides you along the way, and He walks ahead of you.

My wedding day was the most bittersweet day of my life. That morning, my parents and I were enjoying a farewell breakfast. I was emotional about our wedding day and as I wept with my parents, Mom helped me see the next step of the path before me. I knew that God had chosen Tim to be my husband, and I was happy and excited about this great adventure. But I also knew that by marrying Tim, I was leaving my family and my home forever. We were moving to Boston and then eventually to Virginia. I wanted to marry Tim but hated to leave my family in Colorado.

That morning, my mother gave me life-changing wisdom: "Being in the center of God's will is the place of your greatest happiness. You will always be happier with Tim than you would ever be staying here with Dad and me."

She may as well have said, "God has shown you the path for your life. As you trust God and follow Him, you will find great joy and happiness. Go for it!"

Did I see any details of the great adventure that was ahead of me? No! But I knew that God had a path, a plan for me, and I wanted all of what He had for me. There was no better option. But I had to take the next step, go to the church, put on my wedding dress, and walk down the aisle with my sweet daddy. One step at a time, and God's path of life unfolded in front of me. Even after forty years of marriage, this remains true.

This is so important because if we believe God has a path for us, we can ask Him where it is and trust Him to lead us there. If we think God has shown us His path, we need to follow it. What do we have to lose? This path for us is God's very best option. If we make a mistake, God can show us the way. He promises to guide or reroute us. Deuteronomy 30:15–18 shows the distinctive contrast between the path to life and the path to destruction. Once again, we see a clear picture of the ways God loves His people: with compassion, strength, and commitment. He clearly spells out the options for life and death and then provides wisdom for the next step.

The image of the path of life is so concrete and easily understood. It fills me with confidence for new adventures. The promise of fullness of joy—to be completely filled with joy? What could be better than that? And finally, we can be so close to God that we are within His reach, at His right hand, ready to receive from Him. Psalm 16:11 is filled with His promises and direction.

1. God will make the path of life known to us. In His presence we will have fullness of joy.

2. By following God's path, we will be in the center of His will.
3. Our walk with Him will bring us great pleasure (or happiness in the NLV) forever.

As we pay attention to God's leading and communicate with Him often, we will be equipped to stay on the path. Our success happens one step at a time as we watch, depend on, and follow God. God, in His wisdom, often reveals only one step at a time; enough to encourage us, but not so much to burden us. A slower journey probably won't overwhelm us and will build our confidence. If we could see the whole path, our focus would be on the path ahead and not on the one next step and our moment-by-moment dependence on following God's leadership. This wisdom continues to be important in guiding my decisions. I may not always know God's will for my life, but I do know that I will always be happier with the Lord than searching alone to understand the life and steps that are ahead of me. The best way to succeed is to pay attention, listen, follow, and take the next step. These are the reasons this verse guides me.

My own personal L. N. Robertson translation of Psalm 16:11 is, "God has a path, a plan, and a purpose for me every day. He promises to make it known to me, to show me the way, one step at a time. As I journey down God's path for my life, I will be filled with joy—not necessarily happiness, but great joy. I am confident that God is with me and showing me the best way to go. To add to this promise of joy, I will experience God's pleasure and my own, forever. *Forever!*"

What an amazing promise for life. I see it as a "no-lose proposition." God will make it known to me, and if I go with Him, He will bring me joy and eternal pleasure. A close, dependent relationship with God is the eternal pleasure.

Psalm 119:105 declares, "Your word is a lamp to guide my feet and a light for my path." The following chapters will show you the way God shines His light on our paths.

Progress on the path is made when we make the decision to start and then take the first step. So let us begin our great adventure!

Chapter 1

~~~

The First Step on the Path

"I am the way, the truth, and the life. No one
can come to the Father except through me."
—*John 14:6*

As we begin our journey on the path, the first step is an important one and cannot be overlooked. We need a clear understanding of the path maker and guide. Most of us are familiar with the Holy Trinity (Father, Son, and Holy Spirit), but the mystery remains: How do they work together both as separate entities and as three in one? Jesus said, "I am the way, the truth, and the life. No one can come to the Father except through me" (John 14:6). I love the way His words so clearly outline the Trinity and how they work together to help us succeed in our Christian walk. I see them like this:

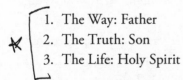

1. The Way: Father
2. The Truth: Son
3. The Life: Holy Spirit

Three separate entities, but one God. I have heard the Trinity explained this way: 1 x 1 x 1 = 1. The word *Trinity* is a compound word using *tri* for three and *unity*. Tri + Unity = Trinity. The Trinity is present throughout the Bible, beginning with the very first verses: "In the beginning God created the heavens and the earth. . . . And the Spirit of God was hovering over the surface of the waters" (Genesis 1:1–2). The narrative continues: "Let us make human beings in our image, to be like us" (Genesis 1:26). Jesus explained:

> "And I will ask the Father, and he will give you another Advocate, who will never leave you. He is the Holy Spirit, who leads into all truth. The world cannot receive him, because it isn't looking for him and doesn't recognize him. But you know him, because he lives with you now and later will be in you." (John 14:16–17)

As I thought more about who God is in my life, my understanding evolved from an awareness of a distant deity to a personal, loving relationship with each component of the Trinity—Father, Son, and Holy Spirit—and all of them became a part of my daily life.

The Way: Knowing the Father

I grew up knowing that God was my heavenly Father. I could sense His love and protection, and like Santa, He knew when I was sleeping, He knew when I was awake, and He knew if I had been bad or good. God and Santa had much in common: they were loving, all-seeing, all-knowing, and generous.

By the time I was nine, my mother had had a deep encounter with Christ. After that experience, she began taking us to a small Episcopal church in Golden, Colorado. Holly Coors, wife of the beer baron, was my Sunday school teacher. I loved Sunday school with her much more than I liked church. She made the Bible come alive, rewarded us for memorizing the books of the Bible, and often brought donuts. Her enthusiasm as a teacher made it worthwhile for me to get up and go to church.

In contrast to other denominations, the teaching of the Episcopal Church doesn't stress inviting Jesus into your heart as your Lord and Savior, so I always believed that if I was an Episcopalian, I would go to heaven. In my ignorance, I believed that if you genuflected as you entered the pew, took communion, and finished with a corporate prayer, you were a Christian. Being "saved" wasn't anything I thought about or even knew about.

Like many young children, I didn't understand my faith, why the congregation did certain things, or what it all meant. By watching everyone else, I learned to bow and make the sign of the cross as I entered and left the pew. Doing that made me feel very religious. In elementary school, the cafeteria served fish on Fridays for the Catholic students. As we went through the line, the lady would ask, "Fish or meat?" I often said fish so my friends would think I was Catholic.

As I grew older, a thought occurred to me: if God is real and if Jesus is God's only Son, I didn't want to miss knowing it. But if all of this isn't true, I didn't want to waste my time. My goal was to make an informed decision about God, not to be ignorant or to have any regrets. I couldn't think of a better place to start than to ask my heavenly Father, "Are You real?" "Is Jesus Your one and only Son?" If God is God, I knew He could handle these questions.

The first time I remember praying was in the fall of my freshman year of college during Parents Weekend. Because I was from Denver and attended Sweet Briar College, a small women's college in Virginia, this was guaranteed to be a lonely weekend. Everyone else was happily united with their parents, and my family was consumed with my older sister, who had to have spinal surgery that same weekend in Denver.

Unhappy, worried, and *lonely* could barely describe my feelings. My roommate was staying in a hotel room with her parents, and for the first time, I was alone in our room. That night I prayed my first earnest prayer: *God, if You love me and if You are my Father, You need to help me. I am so unhappy and want to go home. If this is how You treat Your children, I am not going to believe in You anymore.*

To my great surprise, I felt these words in my soul: *I am your Father, and I do love you. Learn to love Me first, and I will give you more love for your family and friends.*

For the next several months I continued to pray, *Show me who You are; help me to understand Your ways. If You are there, if You can hear me, I want to know You.*

At Christmastime, my sweet father told me he knew I was unhappy at college. He offered to go back to Sweet Briar with me to help me pack my things, return home, and enroll in the University of Colorado. For weeks I had longed to hear those words from him, but to my surprise, instead of feeling happy, I felt defeated. I wanted to conquer this challenge instead of having it conquer me. I didn't want to return home until I didn't feel so defeated by school.

Upon my return to Sweet Briar, two important things happened. First, springtime soon arrived in Virginia. I had never seen such beautiful flowers. The azaleas and dogwood trees displayed their breathtaking colors, and I loved it. The second important thing happened the night I had an urge to pop into the back of the chapel and say thank you to God. Just my going there was another step toward eventually meeting the God who loved me.

In the darkness, I nervously sensed I was not alone. Other people were in the chapel, quietly talking, and I heard one of them say my name. "Lisa? Is that you? What are you doing here?" I couldn't see who was there, but I answered them.

When they finished in the chapel, I left too. In the light, I recognized several of the girls. They explained to me that they met every night at ten o'clock to pray together and invited me to join them.

Ten o'clock at night was not a busy time for me. I was usually available then, so I felt obligated to go back. Having never prayed with anyone other than my mother, and never having prayed out loud, I was a nervous wreck about returning to the prayer group. I knew that when I returned, it would eventually be my turn to actually say a prayer. What is a girl to do? I uttered a quick, silent prayer, *God, please help me to pray out loud, and please give me something to say.* An idea popped into my head, probably something like, "God, I pray for world peace and all the starving children in the world." Not bad for my first time! I prayed aloud and felt greatly relieved. Every night I joined them and pretended to know what I was doing. The other girls assumed I was a Christian. Because of my mother and my childhood church experiences, I knew the words and could speak the language, even if I didn't understand what they really meant.

Summer vacation arrived, and I returned home and continued to think about transferring. One Sunday in June, I went back to my childhood church. Being in a place of prayer helped me realize that I missed my praying friends. My prayer that Sunday morning was, "God, if you want me to believe in You, I need to know who You are. Right now, I am not sure if I believe in You, so if You are real, please help me. Amen."

What I meant was, "This is all so new to me and I don't know what to do to get to know You better. Please help me."

Yes, God does answer prayers. But I was not expecting the kind of answer I received.

It was that summer I met both Jesus the Son and the Holy Spirit. For the first time, the Christian faith made sense to me and I wanted more.

The Truth: Meeting God the Son

Little did I know where that prayer at Calvary Episcopal would lead.

Three days later, I picked up the newspaper at the end of the driveway. Attached to the paper, in a rubber band, was a small flyer with the words, "Jesus Rally tonight. July 6–10. Across from Cinderella City." Jesus rally? My curiosity was piqued.

I had never been to a Jesus rally. Actually, I had never even heard of one. Stained-glass Episcopal churches were my comfort zone. But this sounded intriguing. I called Sylvia, the only Christian friend I had in Colorado, and asked her to go with me. We weren't close, but she was the only person I could think of who might appreciate a Jesus rally. To my surprise, she agreed to go.

The rally was held in a tent that looked as big as a football field. From the parking lot, we heard electric guitars, drums, and a keyboard. Hundreds of people poured into the tent to find their seats on flimsy folding chairs. We soon found ourselves surrounded by worshipping hippies of all ages. The loud rock band played, and the people worshipped with their hands in the air. Long dresses, long hair, beards—and joy. Sylvia and I didn't exactly fit in. And to the people inside the tent, we were a peculiar sight—Top-Siders, short skirts, and sleeveless shirts. Immediately, I knew this night would be interesting! Two sheltered, private-school girls who looked and felt very out of place.

We decided on an aisle seat in case we wanted to make a quick exit. The band continued to play, people sang and danced, and we were intrigued by all that was going on. When the music stopped and the message began, I felt as if I was the only person in the tent and Bill Lowry was speaking just to me. Having a relationship with Jesus was the focus of his message. I had always known God. It was easy—how could anyone not believe in God? At the end of the message, Bill invited anyone who wanted to come to the front of the stage and pray to invite Jesus into their lives. It sounded good to me.

I thought to myself, *Why not? If Jesus is God's Son, I want to know. If this is a waste of my time, I want to know that too. I'm going to give it a try.* Sylvia disappeared, and alone I walked forward to pray with other people and with Bill.

We all prayed together, "Lord Jesus, thank You for loving me. Thank You for dying on the cross for me. Please forgive me for the many mistakes I have made. I ask You to come into my life and teach me to love You and follow You every day of my life. In Jesus' name, amen." Short, sweet, and to the point!

We finished the prayer and I turned to leave the front of the tent. Bill continued, "Now that you have invited Jesus into your lives, would you also like to invite the Holy Spirit?" Being a good Episcopalian, I often crossed myself, or genuflected (as the Catholics do): Father, fingers on my forehead; Son, on my chest; and Holy Spirit, left to right from one shoulder to the other. That was all I knew about the Holy Spirit. Left to right across my chest, after the Father and the Son.

My thoughts were simple: *I know the Father, I just met His Son, Jesus, and I know that the Holy Spirit belongs to the Father and the Son, so why not?*

My traditional Episcopal teaching on genuflecting served me well that night.

Remaining at the stage and watching to see what would be next, I had no way of knowing what to expect.

I thought, *If this is powerful, true, and good, I want it. By experiencing this, I can decide for myself if this faith is for me. Is my faith in God enough, or do I need more?*

The Life: Living with the Holy Spirit

I stood toward the end of the line, waiting my turn for Bill to pray for me. I had never seen anything like this. My experience with the Holy Spirit was almost nonexistent. But I wanted all that God had for me.

Bill came down the line of eager people and randomly put his hands on a few people's heads and prayed for them. I was one of the people for whom he prayed. He placed his hands on my head and to my great surprise, I felt power surge through me; it felt like a waterfall rushing though my body from my head to my toes. I began to cry—not because I felt like a big sinner, not because I was so appreciative, but because I knew I was in the presence of God and had just met Him as the Baptizer. I had never read the Bible or heard a sermon on this; the experience was totally unexpected. Tears were the only way to express what I was feeling.

Bill talked about the possibility of praying in an unknown language. This was also unfamiliar to me and I didn't know what he meant. Bill said that just as a baby learns a new language, we can too. He encouraged us to speak the words on our tongues, so I tried.

Simple sounds, a few syllables, quietly came from my lips. I kept whispering the same strange syllables. Nothing remarkable happened, and I thought, *I am making this up. This makes no sense.* I tried again. Two syllables, then three. Not so impressive. But I wanted to pursue it and wondered, *Is this real? Does it matter? Lord, I want to know if this is worth my time and effort.*

At home that night, I kneeled by my bed and asked, "Lord, is this for real? What just happened to me?" I found my red Bible, which had never been opened since my confirmation at age twelve. Bill had said the Bible was the Word of God, so with childlike faith, I asked, "If this is true, God, will You show me something that will help me?"

Then I flipped it open and found these words:

Now get up and stand on your feet. I have appeared to you to appoint you as a servant and as a witness of what you have seen and will see of me. I will rescue you from your own people and from the Gentiles. I am sending you to them to open their eyes and turn them from darkness to light, and from the power of Satan to God, so that they may receive forgiveness of sins and a place among those who are sanctified by faith in me. (Acts 26:16–18 NIV)

Much like the two disciples who encountered Jesus on the road to Emmaus (Luke 24), my heart burned as I read those words, and the Scripture came alive to me as never before. I had kneeled by my bed and the words in the Bible said, "Stand up!" I had just encountered Christ and the words continued, "I have appeared to you." Could it be that God was speaking to me? Confused and thrilled, I climbed into bed, reflecting on the events of the evening. I didn't know what it all meant, but I knew that God was with me and all of this was true. Filled with peace, I fell asleep.

Like Paul on the road to Damascus, I had a radical, life-changing experience. Words from familiar Christian songs now made sense to me: "I once was lost, but now am found," and "Glory, glory, I saw the light!" and "I have decided to follow Jesus, no turning back, no turning back."

Morning is my favorite time of day. I woke up the following morning and my first thought was, *What happened last night?* I felt as if I had "tied one on" and wondered what I had just done. Was my tent encounter for real? Or had I manufactured the experience and the emotion?

To find the answer, I only had to look out my bedroom window. The sunrise was gold, orange, and pink. Glorious! Something deep in my soul assured me that I had just begun an incredible journey with the God of the universe—all three entities: Father, Son, and Holy Spirit.

With limited knowledge and understanding, I had discovered my first step on the path of life!

Three in One

After a lifetime of searching, for the first time the Father, Son, and Holy Spirit felt unified to me. My childhood faith made sense. I now understood why I genuflected; it was not as an empty action but one of power and holiness. As I crossed myself after a prayer, I felt as if I were asking God the Father, the Son, and the Holy Spirit to cover me with love and protection.

Jesus' words in John 14:6, "I am the way, the truth, and the life. No one can come to the Father except through me," made sense too. Three separate entities, one mighty God.

God the Father—the Creator who loves us. Jesus His Son—who loves us so much that He died for our sins (John 3:16 describes this). And the Holy Spirit—who guides us to experience a vibrant and power-filled life.

I'm no theologian, but when people ask me to describe the Trinity, I describe it this way: God the Father is like our skeleton—He holds us up; God the Son is like our skin—He helps us see His face and recognize Him; and God the Holy Spirit is like our veins, organs, and arteries—He flows through us with life.

Have you heard the popular song from the fifties about what a difference a day makes? Overnight my faith expanded from a simple faith in God to a complete faith in the Trinity—God the Father, God the Son, and God the Holy Spirit.

Without a doubt, twenty-four little hours had drastically changed my life. For years I had asked the Lord, *Where are you? Please help me know your truth.* Never did I imagine that on the night of my "interesting memory" at the Jesus rally, surrounded by hippies, I would begin my journey.

As we enter into a deeper understanding of God the Father, the Son, and the Holy Spirit, our eyes open to see the path, and we discover that the only destination worth walking toward is one that leads to the way, the truth, and the life—the ultimate destination. How can you get there? Ask God to show you His path for you. Be courageous and take the first step and then the next and the next. One step at a time is how you begin the adventure of a lifetime.

An interesting sidenote to my story is that my friend Sylvia, who went to the rally with me, married Grover, the son of Joe and Holly Coors, my fourth-grade Sunday school teacher. I introduced them to each other that week of my conversion, ten years after Holly had been my Sunday school teacher. God is the God of romance! He was at work long before we realized what He was doing! I never realized this "coincidence" until I wrote this chapter.

Chapter 2

~

The Surprising Path

Your road led through the sea,
your pathway through the mighty waters—
a pathway no one knew was there!
—*Psalm 77:19*

Psalm 77 paints a magnificent picture of one of my favorite and most-needed sections of the path: surprises! Surprises always show up at just the right time: never too early and never too late. Often we don't know where or what they are, but when we find the surprises, we discover that they are exactly what we needed and what we needed at exactly the right moment. This path can be difficult to find because God keeps parts of it hidden and we may not be ready for a surprise. If we remember God's faithfulness, we can trust that the path will be made clear in His perfect timing. He will surprise us as only He can.

Surprises on the path are especially important when we are discouraged. A surprise is welcomed if we don't understand our options, if guidance and wisdom are unavailable, or when our progress on the path comes to a halt. It may seem that we are at a standstill, with all roads blocked.

When we feel stuck, God seems quiet and far away. Be careful because we may be tempted to give up. But the promise of surprises encourages us to press forward and keep going. More than once I have discovered that dead ends aren't the end, but often they give me a new opportunity and redirect me to a better way: God's way.

Psalm 77 refers to one of the greatest Old Testament stories, the miraculous parting of the Red Sea. As Moses led the children of Israel from Egypt to the promised land, Pharaoh's army was in hot pursuit. Moses stood at the Red Sea with his people behind him and the enemy army closing in. At the water's edge, God commanded Moses to raise his staff and enter the sea. As he walked into the water, the sea separated and God created a path for Moses and his people.

The Message version of Exodus 14:13 highlights the drama: "Moses spoke to the people: 'Don't be afraid. Stand firm and watch GOD do his work of salvation for you today. Take a good look at the Egyptians today for you're never going to see them again. GOD will fight the battle for you. And you? You keep your mouths shut!'"

With God's specific instructions and the Egyptian army hot on their heels, Moses gained the courage to lead the Israelites into the sea on God's path for them. God said His purpose for the surprising path was "to put my Glory on display so that the Egyptians will realize that I am GOD" (Exodus 14:18 THE MESSAGE). God provided a way of escape for His people not only because He loved them but also because He wanted to demonstrate His power to everyone—both the Israelites and the Egyptians.

This may seem like an excessive demonstration of God's power, but it accomplished what needed to happen—a mighty rescue and deliverance. We are still talking about it and learning from it thousands of years later. It was effective!

Do you think Moses was surprised and relieved to stretch out his hand and watch the seawater part right before his eyes? He overcame any fear of failure because he had few options: to boldly obey God or to be conquered. What did the people think as they watched Moses walk into the sea? Imagine how the children of Israel felt walking through the sea on dry land, with walls of water on both sides of them. Not only does this story have great dramatic and visual details, but it reminds me again of the incredible and unexpected ways that God can answer our prayers and meet our needs. Many times the success of following God's surprising plans comes as we step out and trust Him to lead us. Once again, we see how important our partnership with God is. He has the plans. He doesn't do it for us, and we don't have to be good enough to earn His blessings, but our willingness to partner with Him brings us success. He gets the glory and the credit because we have invited Him into our work.

Even today, God works in unexpected ways for us and continues to astonish us. Throughout our lives we will experience the reality of the surprising path. Because it is a surprise, we might miss it and think of it as a "coincidence" when, in reality, God is showing us His power. I have had a few surprising paths in my life. They are not quite as exciting as Moses' story, but they proved to be powerful and life changing.

For example, my college choice was a surprise. College applications are typically a stressful time for a family. Where to apply? Will they accept me? Will I have any friends? Can I be away from my family for so long or possibly forever? Will I be happy?

In my senior year of high school, I was certain I would live in Colorado for the rest of my life. Colorado is one of the most popular places students choose for college. People from all over the country head to the mountains. Yet, to my surprise, when it came time to make my college decision, I chose to go to a new state. My plan was to spend the rest of my life in Colorado, therefore it seemed like a good idea to begin my college experience somewhere else, so I packed my bags and headed east.

I was taking the opposite path as my parents. Before they moved to Denver, my parents had grown up in different parts of the East Coast, my father in New England and my mother in Pennsylvania. After they graduated college, they each took their own surprising paths that landed them in Denver. Like my parents, I longed for a new experience in another part of the country.

Little did I know that I was well on my way to discovering God's unexpected plan and path for me.

Sweet Briar College (SBC) caught my attention because my favorite teacher had graduated from there. Judy Wilson Grant, my high school English teacher, challenged me to think and to write. Her many funny and memorable stories about her years at Sweet Briar inspired me to go there. I devised a simple plan for college: two years in Virginia, then back to Colorado for my final two years at the University of Colorado.

Throughout the application process, my mother was convinced that God had a plan for me at Sweet Briar. Her confidence gave me the confidence and courage to go to Virginia. I didn't know anyone at Sweet Briar and only knew one other person who was attending college in Virginia. Yet, despite the fear of the unknown, I trusted my mother's words and made the journey eastward, even if I didn't fully understand what she meant.

One of my first memories of SBC was the intense humidity and heat. I had never felt such hot, humid air. Years later my daughter Laura said, "Mommy, the air is *sweaty*!" Humidity, heat, and sweaty air are the same thing.

Cute girls in sundresses welcomed me. I arrived with my backpack and hiking boots, long before anyone on the East Coast wore hiking boots. Hiking boots were my way of protesting the

Lily sundresses. (It wasn't long before I was loving the Lily sundresses too.)

Who knew you could have culture shock just moving from Colorado to Virginia? There was a lot about Sweet Briar I liked, but, as I mentioned earlier, within a few weeks I began to think about my transfer home. The Blue Ridge Mountains were beautiful, but the Rocky Mountains were more my style.

I told myself I would finish my first year and then transfer home to Colorado. Little by little, I saw that my homesickness and feelings of defeat were actually God's way of preparing me for my next step on this path. To my surprise, God was once again at work in my life. The feelings of defeat pushed me to persevere because I didn't want to leave feeling like a failure; I wanted to leave on a more positive note.

College years are so influential. They shape not only how you think but also your lifetime friends, your career, and even where you will live. Surprisingly, I *did* end up staying four years at Sweet Briar and graduated fully confident that, as my mother had said, "God had a plan for me." I grew to love my time at Sweet Briar. Not only did it provide an excellent education, but I learned about hunkering down, even when things were hard, and it was at Sweet Briar where I grew and developed my faith in God.

But the biggest surprise was discovering a love story so perfect it could only have been written by God, and there in the mountains of Sweet Briar, I came to know God as the God of romance.

Through the nightly prayer meetings I discovered my freshman year at Sweet Briar, I became more excited about my faith. I eventually joined the Christian fellowship group and in my junior year was asked to organize the Annual Religious Conference, or ARC, which would happen nine months later. (Yes, the "Annual Religious Conference" was really what it was called. Not some catchy one-word conference name you'd see today, like Equip or Ignite.)

My responsibility was to find a speaker who would spend a weekend at Sweet Briar and (we hoped) inspire the students to discover and grow in their Christian faith. In my mind, this speaker would have to be joyful, inspiring, interesting, smart, challenging, and fun. It seemed as if I asked everyone I knew if they could come and lead this retreat. Understandably, they turned me down because it was not a very attractive offer, but it was the best we had.

"Come to Sweet Briar, the home of fifteen to eighteen Christian girls. Please come for the weekend and speak Friday evening, three times on Saturday, and Sunday morning. We will give you room and board and pay you $400. I continued to pray and ask everyone I could think of. Every potential speaker ran from me—all but one. And when it comes to something like this, one is all you need.

Time was running out. I didn't have any more ideas for a possible speaker other than my last resort, my father. Dad wasn't famous or known as a notable Christian speaker, but I figured that he knew more about the Christian faith than most of my college friends, and he wouldn't turn me down.

But God had another surprise for me.

Three months before the conference and still no speaker, I called home thinking that it might be time to ask Dad to speak. Mom answered the phone and made a shocking announcement: "I have found the speaker for your conference! I read in the paper that a minister from Virginia Beach, with a TV show, was speaking at Calvary Chapel in Denver. To our surprise, he graduated from Yale. Because your father went to Yale, Dad and I were quite curious, so we went to hear him. He was so good, I think he is perfect for Sweet Briar and his name is Pat Robertson." This was a big surprise to me because my parents didn't ever go to Calvary Chapel, but they "happened" to be there on Sunday. Time was running out for me. On just the right day, Pat Robertson was speaking in Denver, but he lived in Virginia. Seemed like a great coincidence to me.

Mom's words intrigued me: "He is a minister from Virginia Beach with a TV show." In those days, every town had ministers on television, but something told me I needed to pursue this.

The following day, I called CBN and spoke with Pat's assistant, Barbara Johnson. I nervously explained who I was and what I wanted. She was gracious and kind. As our conversation continued, she mentioned that Pat had written a book. My response was, "Really? What's the name of the book?"

"*Shout It from the Housetops.* It is the story about his life and the founding of his ministry." Because I had never heard of Pat, I didn't know anything about his book or his TV show, *The 700 Club.* I don't know if she laughed or cried at my ignorance. Years later, Barbara told me that, in all her time working at CBN, she had never had anyone call her to invite Pat to speak who didn't know anything about him. God even had a surprise path for Pat and his wife, Dede.

Barbara asked me to send a letter with the request and promised to review it with her boss. I mailed the letter and ordered *Shout It from the Housetops.* A few days later Barbara called to say that Pat would love to come speak at the Annual Religious Conference. She added that he had "a handsome redheaded son" who attended the University of Virginia and suggested that I invite him also. Barbara was not only Pat's assistant, but also a matchmaker.

I don't remember anything about my final exams that December except that instead of studying, I read Pat's book. If I had known more about him, I never would have invited him, because, by all accounts, he was way out of our league. But God. God is so amazing and full of surprises. I believe God kept me ignorant about Pat so I wouldn't be afraid to invite him to our little Annual Religious Conference tucked away outside of Lynchburg, Virginia. After reading a few pages of his book, I quickly discovered that I had invited a very well-known and popular speaker, and to my shock, he said yes!

Rather than thanking God for this amazing answer to prayer, I was afraid I was in over my head. I was committed, he had committed, and the show must go on. No turning back now.

As I've recounted this story through the years, many people have asked, "Why did Pat say yes?"

Pat was raised in Lexington, Virginia, and graduated from Washington and Lee University, near Sweet Briar (before attending Yale Law School). In his high school and college years, he had dated some women at Sweet Briar, and according to Pat, he had not behaved himself. The family joke is that God sent Pat back to Sweet Briar to do penance for his raucous college years.

The real reason Pat came to Sweet Briar is simple: God called him there, and he obeyed. To this day, I still admire Pat and Dede and their incredible willingness to go where God calls them and to do what He asks. From all appearances, Sweet Briar offered them nothing, but because of their willing hearts, they discovered that God had a new path for them, and with great sacrifice, they followed.

February 13 arrived (it was Friday the 13th). I met the Robertson family in the parking lot: Pat; Dede; their oldest son, Tim; and their youngest daughter, Ann. Instantly, I felt comfortable with Pat and his family. Because I had read his book, I felt as if I already knew them and greatly appreciated their willingness to come. I still couldn't believe that a man of his stature would drive four and a half hours, one way, to speak at our conference.

Most of the fifteen Christian students were on campus. But because Pat was so well-known, other colleges were invited to join our weekend. Another surprise? We had a crowd of several hundred people from the surrounding colleges and the community join us for the weekend.

Pat was more than I had hoped he would be. Inspiring, dynamic, funny, and smart—the perfect combination for a life-changing weekend! Up to that point, I had never heard such rich teaching.

God was on the move at Sweet Briar. Lives were being touched and changed by God. I was thrilled and quite relieved. The weekend was a success in every way, including my introduction to Pat's "handsome redheaded son."

I would love to tell you that Tim jumped at the chance to leave Charlottesville for a Christian conference with his parents and younger sister. But the truth was, his parents insisted that he come. Like his father, Tim had spent some time at Sweet Briar and wasn't known as a Christian leader; he was better known for being a good dancer and a fun date.

When his parents asked Tim if he would go with them, Tim tried to convince them that he had too much work to do. Tim was naturally smart, and schoolwork had never been his first priority, until that weekend.

His father responded that they would pick him up at 4:00 p.m. This command performance was out of character for all of them. Reluctantly, Tim arrived on campus with his family.

Tim was known as a little bit of a party boy and didn't want to come because he thought he might discredit his father. When Tim showed up with his father, however, just the opposite happened. My friends all knew Tim as one of the lively ones at UVA, and because of this, they instantly liked him. Their reaction was that if Pat had a great son like Tim, Pat must be okay. And again, we see that the Lord works in mysterious ways, full of surprises around every corner!

At the close of the weekend, Pat concluded the Sunday morning message with an invitation for the students to come forward and pray to receive Christ. Together, Tim and I helped pray with the people who came forward. Another little surprise was that one of the girls we prayed with turned out to be the niece of one of Pat's good friends and former CBN board member.

The weekend following the conference, Sweet Briar hosted a

winter dance. Naturally, at a women's college, the women do the inviting for their formal dances. By the end of the conference, several of my friends wanted to invite Tim to the dance, and I did too.

I didn't want to be rude to my friends, and I didn't want to miss this great opportunity, so I put the burden on the Lord: *Lord,* I prayed, *if You want me to ask Tim, I ask that You would give me an opportunity to be with him alone, preferably before one of my friends decides to invite him.* When it comes to prayer, it never hurts to be specific!

Would it surprise you to know that I did get some time alone with him? As his parents packed, Tim and I were outside, waiting to load their car. It seemed to take them forever to pack. Eventually, I got up the nerve and invited him to go with me. He graciously and enthusiastically accepted my invitation.

Tim remembers driving with a friend down to Sweet Briar for the dance and saying, "Crabtree, I don't know. This girl could be trouble. She is not like the rest."

When we arrived at the dance, I wasn't sure what to expect. I mistakenly assumed that a preacher's kid probably didn't do much dancing. Another surprise? We never left the dance floor, and he was one of the best dancers out there.

The next week, we drove together to a small house church. On our way, I was struggling to control my excitement about Tim and how much fun it was to go to church with him. Joy and love filled my heart; my feelings amazed me. On the car ride, my Bible was on my lap, so I quietly asked the Lord if He might give me a scripture that would help me understand this new relationship. I flipped open the Bible and my eyes fell on these words: "O magnify the LORD with me, and let us exalt His name together" (Psalm 34:3 NASB).

Closing the Bible, I knew we would always be good friends.

Springtime arrived again in Virginia, and love was in the air! Tim and I saw each other as often as we could and talked on the phone in between visits. It was several weeks of whirlwind dating, and I found myself praying, *Lord, please have Tim tell me that he loves me, because if he doesn't, I might accidentally blurt out "I love you" first. That wouldn't be the way it is supposed to be.*

I know there may be readers who disapprove of the speed of this, but we were graduating in six weeks, and I was moving home to Denver, so there was a little urgency for us to discover what we had in this new romance.

After a month, he did tell me he loved me.

Weeks after our first date, I learned more about Tim's original plans for the weekend of my dance. Tim had invited a girl to visit him at UVA on the same weekend as our dance. After he accepted my invitation and returned to UVA, he tried to figure out how he would manage two women he had agreed to accompany on Friday night.

I don't know if he asked God to help him out, but to his relief (and mine), God stepped in. On Wednesday before the dance, Tim received a phone call from the other girl explaining that she had a paper to write and couldn't come to UVA that weekend.

The spring of our senior year flew by, and before we knew it, I was on my way back to Denver. We wrote letters and talked on the phone once a week (times have changed!). We saw each other as often as we could. Living in Virginia and Colorado was a challenging way to date.

One August night at his family's house, Tim asked me to marry him. The most memorable line of his eloquent proposal was, "I can't afford to date you." He thought he could afford to marry me, but not date me. It still makes me laugh.

I said yes—and life with Tim continues to be filled with many surprising paths.

After five months of marriage, we moved to Boston. From September to December, Tim worked to launch a new TV station.

In January he started a three-year master of divinity program at Gordon-Conwell Theological Seminary in South Hamilton, Massachusetts.

I spent the fall doing part-time work for a printer and interviewing for jobs with Boston companies—General Electric, Polaroid, and Raytheon. The fall changed to winter without any promise of a job offer. As January approached, I began to panic; soon, Tim would stop working and start school. I had to have a full-time job. Of course, God knew this, but I reminded Him constantly. As a last resort, I applied to the seminary for an exciting position as a clerical worker in their bookstore, earning minimum wage, and they offered me the job!

Graciously, I responded to the job offer with a spiritual, "Thank you so much. Please let me pray about it and get back to you by Thursday afternoon." *Click.* Instantly, my fervent prayers began. *Thank You for answering our prayers for a job. But is this the best job You have for me? Please, God! Maybe You have something a little more interesting?* I didn't want to be ungrateful, but clerical work for minimum wage was not the reason I'd gone to college. I had prayed for a job and hoped to find one in Boston. Challenges, excitement, new experiences, and, of course, a higher salary wouldn't hurt. After all, I had a lot of new responsibilities and a new student husband to support!

Thursday afternoon I prayed: *"Lord God, I will go where You want me to go and take whatever job You have for me. You love me and You know what is best for me! Please show me Your path and I will follow You."*

I was reminded of Psalm 16:11, the scripture that anchored my heart: "You will make known to me the path of life; in Your presence is fullness of joy; in Your right hand there are pleasures forever" (NASB). How could I not trust God when He had given me a promise like that?

A ringing phone broke the quiet of my desperate prayers. I answered it, and to my surprise there was an unfamiliar voice on the other end.

"Hello, Lisa? This is Jim Mulcahy from Polaroid. Several months ago, you applied for a job. I have read your résumé, talked to everyone who has interviewed you, and I know you are perfect for this job. We need someone to work in customer service, a temporary job that should last about six months. The only thing I need to do is meet you. The job starts Monday. Can you come to my office tomorrow and we will get all the paperwork done?"

The job started on Monday, and Tim started school on Monday. Was this for real? Only God.

If I could have run to Cambridge that minute to accept the job, I would have. Shock, joy, and excitement filled my grateful and relieved heart. (Tim's too!)

There were a few details that escaped me, like the reality of the commute: It began with a fifteen-minute walk to the train station in Beverly Farms, then a forty-five-minute train ride into Boston, then a connection to the Red Line to Cambridge, and, finally, a one-and-a-half-mile walk from Kenmore Square to Memorial Drive to the historic Polaroid building. Total travel time? At least one and a half hours one way. No problem! I had the job. Every once in a while, I drove to work. Traffic in and out of Boston was terrible, so the train commute was a good option. I didn't mind that it took three hours out of my day.

To this twenty-three-year-old with her first "grown-up job," it was perfection. The commute was a delight to me. And God also came through with the finances; my salary was $1,000 a month, no benefits. I was going to make more money than if I had worked at the bookstore. Just in the nick of time. The God of the midnight hour.

The job was so much fun and the people even better. At that

time, Polaroid was on the cutting edge of instant photography, and its innovative products were constantly evolving.

In the winter, however, the long, cold commute became a burden. Six months passed, and the temporary job was ending. It was time for God to come through with the next step on the path of surprises. My hope and prayer was to have a permanent job secured before I left to visit my family in Denver for a few weeks.

One of my favorite prayers is "We do not know what to do, but our eyes are on you" (2 Chronicles 20:12 NIV).

Lord, I prayed, *You have a path and a plan for me. Please show me the next step. Please help me to have an open mind and heart as You lead me.*

As I navigated the afternoon traffic, praying for God to show me what to do, I noticed a car and a well-dressed woman on the side of the highway. For some reason, I stopped to help her. I offered her a ride, and she looked relieved to have someone come to her rescue. It was a short ride to the gas station, fewer than ten minutes, but those minutes changed my life. We made small talk about her car and the weather. One of her final questions was, "Where do you work?" I proudly told her that I was at Polaroid, but the commute was too much and my six months were coming to an end, so I was looking for a new job.

As she exited my car at the gas station, she handed me her card and asked me to come see her the next day. Her card read, "Rita Brown, Playbill and Panorama Magazines, CEO and Publisher."

What had just happened, and what would it mean?

Fifteen minutes before, I had been minding my own business, trying to navigate afternoon traffic on Route 128, and now I had a random job interview?

"What a difference a day makes. Twenty-four little hours." Tony Bennett sings it, and it accurately describes so much of my life.

The next day I found myself sitting in Rita's office in downtown

Boston. After a pleasant conversation, to my delight and surprise, she said, "I publish and own two magazines. *Playbill* is the theater guide for all the major Boston theaters, and *Panorama* is the leading tourist magazine, placed in almost every hotel room in the city.

"These magazines are totally dependent on advertising. I have one man who has handled all the advertising for the past eight years, and I want to hire another person. I will match your Polaroid salary, and when you sell enough ads, I will put you on commission. The harder you work, the more money you can make. The theater season will begin in a few weeks, and I want you to start as soon as you return from your visit to Denver."

Shocked and thrilled, I thought, *What just happened? Did I really hear those words?* I left her office with a song in my heart and the confidence that, once again, God had a plan and a path for me. As I paid attention to Him and kept an open heart and mind, He was showing me my way, which was actually *His* way. "Thanks be to God for his indescribable gift!" (2 Corinthians 9:15 NIV).

What an incredible opportunity! Ad sales in Boston! My great-grandfather had started one of the first ad agencies in Boston. This was all part of my DNA. Opportunity, hard work, and downtown Boston were in my hands, all because I had stopped to help a stranded woman. (That was the only time in my life I had stopped to help someone on the side of the road.)

The reality of the job was hard, hot work in an old, awful building in the south end of Boston. The commute was better than the long Polaroid train ride and walk, but my office wasn't air-conditioned, the elevator barely worked, and the one salesman who had the job by himself was not excited about my arrival. I was now his competition, hungry and chasing down new business.

For the publishers, hiring me was a great idea because Jack had become very comfortable in his job as the lone salesman, and now he had some competition. For me, it was a great opportunity to learn how to sell advertising, to discover the city of Boston, and to get a lot of exercise. I walked almost all day, every day. I would leave the house before seven in the morning and walk to the train. (We had only one car, and Tim needed it for school.) The train from Beverly Farms took me to North Station; then I transferred to the underground and rode to South Station; then I walked across the bridge on Summer Street to my old, hot office. I loved it and every day learned about life, God, and Boston.

More than once I was able to get appointments with very important ad executives to tell them about Rita's amazing magazines. I would go through all the benefits of buying ads with *Playbill* and *Panorama*. The execs would stare at me and in their confusion say, "*PlayBILL* magazine? I thought you worked for *PlayBOY* magazine!" I was always quick to clear that up, but those men rarely bought ads.

"This is what the LORD says—your Redeemer, the Holy One of Israel: 'I am the LORD your God, who teaches you what is good for you and leads you along the paths you should follow'" (Isaiah 48:17).

A Divine Interruption

Sometimes the surprising path can come in the form of divine interruption. In today's world, so often we move at lightning speed from one thing to the next, and I'm convinced that the tiny screens we grip in our hands are giving us all some form of attention deficit disorder. We have voices, images, and texts coming at us from all sides. But God. Even in the noise and the hustle, He is moving. Even in the middle of our busiest, craziest moments, He has things to do. Our job is to slow the pace, quiet the noise, and listen. And when we do, once again, we see that He is full of surprises along the path.

Another life-changing surprise happened years after we moved from Boston to Virginia Beach. Family life was so busy and I felt as if I was always late to something. I had been to the bank and had one last stop at the grocery store to pick up a few essentials for a quick meal.

This early December evening, the sun was setting, the air was chilly, and as I ran into the store, I grabbed a cart and bolted through the door.

Out of the corner of my eye, I saw a woman standing outside the door with her young daughter beside her. It was too cold for anyone to be outside for very long, but they were there, not asking for money, just waiting for something. It seemed odd to me.

Entering the store, I clearly heard God's gentle voice, *"Give them $100."* At first it was easy to ignore this request. The woman wasn't asking for money, she hadn't spoken to me, and I would feel so strange just butting into her life and giving her money. Yet the voice in my heart continued, *"Give her $100."* I had just been to the bank and happened to have some crisp bills in my purse.

I was too hurried to be bothered, but I knew enough to know that if I didn't give them the money, I would regret it and wouldn't stop thinking about it. The Lord continued to ask me to give them the money. I left my cart in the produce section and headed out the door to find the mother and child. Yes, they were still out in the cold, still waiting.

I walked up to her with a one-hundred-dollar bill in my hand and said, "God has heard your prayers and He asked me to give this to you. Please know how much He loves you. God has a plan for your life and He wants to give this to you."

Feeling so awkward, we both smiled and she said, "Thank you."

Back to the cart and my important grocery list, I continued to get a few things.

After I checked out, I happened to exit the store with the same woman and child. The young mother hugged me, said thank you again, and we went our separate ways. It was an unusual and peculiar event, but I was relieved that I'd done what I'd thought God was asking me to do. In the months that followed, when I thought about this unusual encounter, I would pray for the mother and daughter.

About a year and a half later, I was asked by a church to lead a group of inner-city women and introduce them to an initiative I was involved with called Faithful Beginnings. Faithful Beginnings was created to combine important kindergarten school readiness milestones with basic faith truths, scriptures, and activities for parents to do with their children at home. This church had created a program for children one to five years old to equip mothers with the tools to reinforce these school readiness ideas.

Through my work with Faithful Beginnings, I learned that 90 percent of a child's brain is developed by the time the child turns five. The early years might be the most strategic time to teach children how to learn. Reading and math were not our focus; school readiness was. We emphasized helping them learn how to learn.

For example, we helped the children recognize different shapes, colors, words, and sizes. We encouraged them to notice the beauty of nature, the sun, and the seasons. Speaking in complete sentences was also important. As the teachers taught the basics to the children, I worked with their parents to help them learn how to do the follow-up work with their children and blend school readiness principles with faith foundations.

One day, as the children learned about Noah and the animals, I taught the parents about Noah with a different emphasis: that God had a plan and a purpose for Noah. As Noah partnered with God and followed God's directions, God had a promise for Noah.

As He did for Noah, God also has a plan for us; as we pray to, partner with, and follow God, we will discover God's plans, promises, and purposes for us. The *p* words made the lesson easier to remember. Pray, partner, participate, and pursue the plans, promises, and purposes.

As I taught about God's plan and purpose for Noah, a woman raised her hand and interrupted me. "Excuse me! I have a testimony. Can I tell my testimony? I have a testimony." She was new and I wasn't sure what to expect from her.

My first thought was, *I am giving a good teaching here! Let's wait and hear your testimony after I finish.* But instead I said, "Yes, please tell us your testimony." I was curious to hear her.

The woman, who we'll call Millie, began, "Last year, I didn't have enough money to pay our electric bill. I was standing outside Farm Fresh because a friend told me that he would meet me there and give me some money to pay my bill before the electric company turned off my electricity. I went to Farm Fresh with my daughter and waited and waited, but he never showed up. Just as I was about to give up, a woman ran into the store, and a few minutes later, she came out and spoke to me. 'God has a plan and a purpose for you. He has heard your prayers and asked me to give this money to you. God bless you.' She placed some money into my hand and ran back into the store. I opened my hand and there was $100. This was exactly what I needed to pay the electric bill."

As Millie told the story, my eyes filled with tears.

"Millie, I was the woman who gave you the money."

I am not sure who was more shocked, Millie or me. She burst into tears and ran to hug me.

Almost every woman there began to cry at this incredible God story. When I first saw Millie, it was winter. We were both in coats and hats. Neither one of us realized that we had first met more than a year before.

There were so many miracles and blessings that day. But the one that still stands out to me is that months earlier God had prepared this meeting between Millie and me. Because of our chance encounter, God made Himself known to all the women there. It was so clear that God had a plan for Millie and me. Her story gave me credibility with a group of women who were skeptical toward God and me. This gave me a deep sense of God's plan and purpose for all of us. They felt it too. We were all exactly where we needed to be. We needed to be together, learning about God's great love, faithfulness, miracles, and plans for us.

Several months later, Millie gave me a note that remained in my wallet for years. "Thank you so much. You are a great person and woman of God. We need more people like you in this world. I can't repay you in money, but I can repay you in love and prayer. God bless your grandkids. Love you always, Millie."

In so many ways, I received much more than I gave. Isn't that just like God? What if I hadn't heeded His voice and chosen to listen to Him and do what He was asking me to do? God would have probably found another way to provide for Millie, but I would have missed out on being a part of God's surprising miracle for both of us. Tuning out the distractions of the day is always a challenge. From this, I learned that when it comes to hearing God's voice, I never want to be so busy or distracted that I miss His great adventures for me. When we tune in to the voice of God with a willingness to do what He asks, we are ready for the great surprises He has prepared for us!

~~~~~~

Generations of people have seen that life on God's path is full of unexpected miracles. The Bible is full of great stories of God surprising His people. Moses was surprised to find a pathway no one knew was there—dry land through the Red Sea. Adam was surprised by Eve, Joshua must have been surprised when the walls came tumbling down, and Mary was surprised when the angel

Gabriel visited her. These are just a few examples of the best-known surprises. None of my stories are as dramatic, but they still remind me of God's great love for us. Over and over, He perfectly weaves the most beautiful stories together to demonstrate His power, presence, and love. God's path for His people is not only creative and unique, but it is also filled with surprises.

Chapter 3

~~~

The Difficult Path

You crown the year with a bountiful harvest;
even the hard pathways overflow with abundance.
—*Psalm 65:11*

September 17 is coming again. It comes every year—year after year.

We all have a birthday, and we celebrate it once every 365 days. We never forget when it is, and hopefully our loved ones don't either. Yet, one of those 365 days is also the day of our death, a "deathday." We pass it year after year but never know when it is or when that day will become significant to us or to those we love. September 17 is one of those days.

Growing up in the foothills of the Colorado mountains provided the backdrop for an idyllic childhood. Our family lived in a community of one hundred homes and acres of land. Our winter entertainment was a little ski hill that was probably timbered by the hearty fathers of years gone by. Saturday mornings were filled with lugging our skis and paraphernalia down to the ski hill for a lesson. Up and down the small hill was our weekly routine. The climb always seemed to take forever, and the run down lasted only seconds, literally seconds. Tennis, swim team, and biking filled our time when we weren't skiing or riding horses. Too good to be true is usually too good to be true.

September 17 arrived during the transition between riding bikes and skiing. My brother had an after-school activity, so Mom picked us up and took us home. On this day, Mom arrived at school in her navy blue convertible. She was fit, athletic, beautiful, and always tan. Laura, my little two-and-a-half-year-old sister, bounced around in the backseat. Believe it or not, this was the era when no one had heard of car seats or seat belts. My first-grade brother, Sherlock; one of his friends; and I rode with her. The top was down, the air was crisp, and life was good.

As we arrived home, my mother and Sherlock went downstairs, his friend was sent home, I watched TV, and Laura went out the back door to play in her sandbox. It seemed like an ordinary day, but everything in our world exploded when Jennifer, my older sister, walked through the door and said, "Laura is taking a nap in the sandbox." This didn't seem bad to me because Laura hadn't napped that day. My mother, however, instinctively knew something was seriously wrong. Two-year-olds don't just nap in the sandbox. Bolting out the door, she found Laura facedown in the sandbox. "Call for help! Call the Browns for help!"

The neighbors quickly arrived, and Mom carried a limp Laura into the back of a car and rushed her down the mountain to the children's hospital. Another neighbor arrived at our house and nervously gathered us together and took us to her home for what became the longest night of my life. Dinner was followed by some lame games and artificial conversation.

Jennifer, Sherlock, and I stayed up waiting for my parents to come home with Laura. Finally we heard their car and jumped up to greet them. I can still remember their somber faces as they walked into the room. With forced smiles, they hugged us, but their bodies were stiff, and life suddenly felt so different. Everything had changed.

"Come, children. Let's all sit down." This was a bad sign, because we were still at the neighbor's house, and it was past our bedtime. We huddled together and the icy words were spoken: "Laura is in heaven now; she is living with God. She won't be with us anymore," followed by a flood of tears.

I don't think there are words in the English language that could accurately describe this. *Surreal, grief, numb, devastated,* and *confused* all barely scratch the surface. Mom and Dad attempted to be strong for us, not realizing that none of us had the ability to process our emotions or to understand what had just happened.

My siblings and I all slept in the same room that night. At least we still had each other. Morning came and more neighbors arrived to help by feeding us breakfast. When I first opened my eyes, I looked forward to the day ahead of me, but seconds later, I had a sinking sense that something terrible had happened and life was never going to be the same.

The following days were a blur, and I have no clear memory of them other than Laura's funeral, which was held at our beautiful mountain community church. I didn't want to go, so my parents let me stay with my friend Mary. I was relieved to be with her until I looked out her living room window and realized I could see the church from her beautiful home on top of Tower Hill. My mind took a permanent snapshot of all the cars, the people, and the church. As hard as I tried, I could not escape the reality of Laura's death. Because the pain in my heart was so deep, I tried hard to convince myself that I never loved her. Maybe if I hadn't really loved her, I wouldn't hurt so much.

Mom and Dad seemed like zombies as they moved through the following weeks. Daily, we all tried to live, but *survive* is a more accurate word. The questions persisted. What happened? How did Laura die? And when we thought it couldn't get worse, another bomb hit our family.

Several weeks later, our minister came to the house to talk to us. We gathered for some small talk, which eventually led to the subject of Laura's death. The minister told us that an autopsy had been done so we could try to understand what had happened to Laura. We all listened. "Small handprints and some bruises were found over her mouth." This was not news to my parents, but they wanted the minister to deliver this to us because they couldn't. Someone had come into our perfect world and done the unthinkable. I suspected that night who that someone was.

My brother's friend was told to go home, but maybe he lingered. We never imagined he'd intended to kill her but when he was with her something could have happened, ending in her death.

Our pediatrician called my mother to say that he couldn't tell her the boy did it, but he could tell her that the boy was capable of doing it because he had so much darkness inside of him. He told her what she already knew in her heart. She never had any doubt that the boy killed Laura, and the doctor's call confirmed her beliefs.

My devastated parents scheduled a meeting with his parents to talk to them about Laura's death. My parents had lost their daughter, and they hoped they could help the boy and his family. They knew he should get counseling. No one thought about pressing charges against the child for murder. This was never an issue and never discussed. The authorities were never contacted. Even the hospital where the autopsy was performed didn't contact the authorities. In this small community, we were like family. This was a different era than today. Informing the parents and wanting to help the boy was the point of the meeting. It did not go well. My parents were called liars, crazy, and worse. Instead of helping their son, his parents went into denial.

As a family, we cried together during the first year. Into the second year, the tears subsided. We understood this was our new normal and we had to live with it. September 17 was always a day of tears, as was Laura's birthday. I buried her memory as deep as possible and hardened my heart to the pain. Unbeknownst to me, Mom had been observing me through the years and thought I had not grieved appropriately. Maybe she noticed that I lived as if Laura had never existed. I pushed the pain deeper until I felt as if I was almost free of it. I never felt the need to discuss any of this because her death was so hard for me to accept and almost seemed as if it hadn't really happened.

For my parents, the best way to fight the grief was to have another baby as soon as possible. To their great joy, within months after Laura's death, Mom was pregnant. Hope, celebrations, and a new future filled our home. Eleven months after the worst time in our lives, our family joyfully welcomed Barbara Sears Nelson. She was, and still is, everyone's favorite, and her arrival gave us a new reason to live—especially for my mother. Barbara was a perfect, beautiful, and happy baby. Her presence was God's way of helping all of us focus on living and loving. Her birth gave us the confidence that life was beginning again.

Jennifer and I both wanted to be Barbara's mother, and Sherlock was her protective and adoring older brother. Barbara's life gave Mom life. Watching Barbara grow, learn to walk, ride horses, and go to school filled Mom with a renewed sense of purpose. After all, Barbara was named after my mother (although Mom went by Babby). For Dad, her arrival gave him the opportunity to be the best father. He could redo some things that he hadn't done as well when we were younger. And he did. Jennifer was eleven, Sherlock was seven, and I was nine, and the whole family had a new life to love.

For many reasons, Barbara was God's gift to each one of us. Her life brought us a renewed strength and new hope for the future.

Looking back, I am surprised that none of us were afraid to love her or afraid to lose her. Eventually we returned to a more normal life.

With Barbara's arrival, the prevailing attitude of the community was, "The Lord gives and the Lord takes away. It's okay, they have a new sister now." But we knew that it wasn't quite that simple. Life moved on and we tried to keep up. The stress of the neighborhood gossips, however, took its toll on our family, especially on my mother.

In her memoirs written for her children and grandchildren, Mom retells a life-changing moment:

The children were in school. I was home alone and the phone rang. It was a friend, neighbor, and psychiatrist. He cruelly proclaimed that our child was dead and nothing could be done about it, but now (the boy's) mother was in a mental hospital. He told me that if I didn't write her a letter to tell her that I was mistaken, that I would have two deaths on my hands, hers being the second one. The request was impossible to fulfill.

I hung up the phone, put my head down on the kitchen counter, and cried out, "Oh, God, help me!" Suddenly, my kitchen was flooded with a brilliant light and powerful presence. I knew that the Lord was there and in the moment of my greatest anguish, God had taken it away and washed me with the greatest peace that I have ever known. I just sat there, thanking Him.

None of us knew it at the time, but with this peculiar experience, our family started a brand-new journey. The strange peace that filled Mom was noticeable. Each week women came to be with her. Often they invited her to go with them to a weekly healing service at a small Episcopal church. As they left, they always promised to pray for her and the family.

The prayers of her friends gave Mom new hope and strength.

Through them, Mom eventually encountered the life-changing power of Christ. She experienced His powerful "peace that passes all understanding" long before she knew what it meant to be a Christian (Philippians 4:7). Her friends' prayers and ministry restored her shattered heart and gave her reasons to live again. Of course life would never be the same. We would never, ever understand the whys about Laura's death, but we still had to keep on living, and prayer helped Mom do that.

To help me cope, I turned to tennis, field hockey, and skiing. As I grew older, I loved my social life and worked very hard to keep up with it. High school faded into the beginning of college, and soon I was on my way to Sweet Briar. Before I left for college, Mom and I had the typical mother-daughter going-away-to-college talk. Eventually the conversation turned from the dangers of college life to a subject that we hadn't discussed in a long time, Laura's death.

"If I hadn't found the forgiveness of Christ, I would have killed myself," were Mom's words that began to unravel my heart. Mom, the rock of my life, the one I had watched survive the most heinous experience I could imagine, just revealed to me that she had thought about killing herself. I remembered the days when her heart was so broken and confused that it seemed to me she lived an inch at a time. "God, please help me" was a prayer I'd heard Mom utter as she coped with her loss.

"Why would you ever do that?" was my stunned response. This all seemed impossible to me. She answered, "The guilt of Laura's death is why. If I had done something, it never would have happened. Maybe I could have prevented it? I have never gotten over it." I was shocked. How could she have ever felt responsible? I was the one closest to Laura.

"No, Mom," I blurted out. "Maybe it was my fault. You were busy. I was in the house too."

I don't know who was more taken aback. For years I had wondered if maybe it was my fault. The startling revelation that she had thought about ending her life, combined with the realization that she was carrying the same grief and guilt that I carried, sent me reeling. Ten years after Laura's death, I heard about my mother's suicidal thoughts, her burden of responsibility, and found out that in her grief she had discovered the love of God and was set free by the power of His forgiveness.

Her lingering words, "If I hadn't found the forgiveness of Christ," resonated in me for months to come. My mother had just sent me a life raft, and I needed to figure out what that meant.

Please understand, after ten years and adolescence, I was not dwelling on Laura's death. I had successfully buried the pain and moved on to live a happy teenage life. This conversation, however, awakened the hunger and motivated me to search for the same healing and freedom my mom had experienced. In God's perfect timing, very slowly something was happening in my life too. I began to see glimpses of God's presence, faithfulness, and miracles—small glimpses, but they were real.

I remembered how in the years following Laura's death Mom changed. She navigated the grief in different ways: most notably through her new interest in Bible studies and church. She prayed about everything and would share the answers to her prayers—never too much, but always just enough. Previously a broken and devastated woman, eventually she became one of the first women of her time to launch an international business. God changed her. He gave her a revolutionary idea and the confidence, strength, and tools to succeed in the new venture. Today Ski and Sea International continues to thrive and grow. Now it is under the leadership of my sister Jennifer.

Many of life's great questions lingered for me. Laura was probably killed by someone we knew. Where was God? How could He have allowed this tragedy, an innocent life stolen, a young family devastated? It was confusing. God could have prevented this, but He didn't. But in the midst of a devastating tragedy, God brought my mother new reasons to live. Yes, He is the Lord of the resurrection. He brings life from death, and now I could see my mother with a new outlook on life. Even if God didn't prevent Laura's death, I saw Him use it to minister to many through my mom.

And Mom's story of healing continued to unfold. Yes, she had found forgiveness in her newfound life in Christ. Genuine freedom and peace were evident. Not only had she been healed by Christ's forgiveness, but in the months that followed, God asked for more. He asked her to extend that same forgiveness to the boy we believed had stolen Laura's life. "Impossible!" was her immediate response. She couldn't do that.

To me, this is one of the most powerful aspects of our story. Now Mom was faced with the almost unimaginable challenge of extending the supernatural forgiveness that she'd received from God to the one who had sent her on this terrible journey. She had every right to be hateful and bitter. What happened was wrong and unfair. Hating seemed to be the only appropriate response.

Hatred and bitterness can lock us in a private emotional prison. Mom knew that she had been challenged by God to forgive, and not just to forgive the boy in her heart but to his face. Wisely, she placed the burden on God: *If you set this up and give me the opportunity, I will extend forgiveness to him. God, I am willing, but You must help me. I can't forgive him without You giving me Your forgiveness. I don't have forgiveness for him.* She was willing to forgive, and God was ready to guide her.

One summer day, Mom looked out her window and happened to see the boy walking by himself. She knew this was the moment to do what she had promised God. She stepped outside and called to him. He stopped. He must have been afraid of what she might say to him.

To her surprise, the simple words came from her mouth, "[His name], I love you. And I forgive you." She hadn't planned on what to say, but God gave her those simple words of love. Stunned, he gave her an awkward little smile and ran home. She was as surprised by the words as he was. Because she'd trusted God to lead her through this valley, Mom had experienced God's miraculous joy and a new freedom.

From Mom's memoirs, she concludes this part of her story with these words: "I realized at that moment that forgiveness is a gift from God. I don't believe that we can make ourselves forgive someone. I believe that the Lord gives us the forgiveness. He does it through us."

The gift of forgiveness was a life raft sent by God to rescue my mother, and eventually, it rescued me too. Forgiveness has been one of the greatest gifts and greatest hurdles in my life.

I watched the miracle of forgiveness heal my mother. Mom was able to forgive because she was willing to do what God had asked her to do. She yielded to the Lord and asked for His help, His timing, and His strength. God did the hard part: He gave her healing, freedom, strength, and peace. In her deep grief, Mom was set free by the work of God. She asked for God's forgiveness, and she generously extended God's forgiveness to the boy. It's interesting to me that she gave him God's forgiveness, not her own. After she received forgiveness, she then had the God-given resources to obediently forgive. The boy never asked for forgiveness, but Mom was willing and ready, simply because God had asked her to forgive. Her obedience to God's challenge brought her a miraculous healing, another miracle on this difficult path.

As children, we knew that Mom's Christian life changed her,

because we watched it happen. Forgiveness received and then forgiveness given took my mother from the prison of death and placed her into the land of the living. Day by day, she walked in a new freedom, determined to continue to live her life and help us live ours as normally as possible. Words from the Bible fortified her and taught her how to survive. She trusted God to lead her in the path of life, and He did.

Had she not made the decision to trust God and all that He offered her, I think our family may have been destroyed. We all struggled and reacted very differently to Laura's death. The biggest change for all of us was the influence of Mom's faith in God. Continually, she talked about God's presence in her life. Dad became more aware of his family. His attention changed from being focused on his social life to taking a greater interest in his children. My parents' marriage was reinforced through this tragedy and their newly found faith. It took Dad a few years longer to find his faith, but when he finally did, we all saw a change.

The Power of Forgiveness on the Difficult Path

Most of us have suffered great pain and have reasons to be bitter, angry, hurt, or disappointed. Jesus' simple teaching, however, continues to bring healing: "Love your enemies and pray for those who persecute you" (Matthew 5:44 NIV). These are some of the tools that help us live triumphant lives, not lives weakened by debilitating sin and unforgiveness. There is no reason to live in the prison of bitterness and unforgiveness when the God of the universe provides our way out.

To forgive can be challenging, but with God's help it can also be life changing. Forgiveness is one of God's greatest gifts to His people. There is tremendous power in the gift of forgiveness. God forgives us and then challenges us to forgive those who have hurt and persecuted us. This can be a miraculous work. As we receive God's forgiveness, we will be equipped to forgive others with the same God-given forgiveness. It is so difficult, but forgiveness leads us to the path of freedom. When we experience God's forgiveness, we receive His healing.

Receiving God's forgiveness also helps us to experience His deep love. Once again, we see where we are in partnership with the Lord. He doesn't simply erase the pain; we go to Him, ask for forgiveness, and receive this miraculous gift. The healing that comes from forgiveness can be complete and happen in an instant, or it can be a gradual process. Each person and circumstance is different. When we walk in the freedom of both being forgiven and forgiving others, we gain some of the tools needed to live healthy lives. It is always our choice to receive forgiveness and then to extend it. God leads us on our path but never forces us to do what we need to do.

Watching my parents' hearts heal from Laura's death was a slow and steady process. They didn't heal themselves; God healed their broken hearts and restored hope to them.

One experience that helped me understand the healing process of forgiveness was a time when I fell off a bicycle. My daughter had been riding carelessly in front of me and the back wheel of her bicycle hit my front wheel. I lost my balance and bounced along the pavement, trying to keep the bike up, but I fell on the side of the road. Not only did I tear my best jeans, but I had a ten-inch scrape on my left arm.

The healing of my scrape became a picture of forgiveness. The superficial edges of my wound healed quickly, just like some types of forgiveness—quickly healed and forgotten. But weeks later, the healing continued and the wound got smaller and my ten-inch injury diminished to just an inch. This little remaining wound may have been small, but it was also a very deep cut and it took a long time to heal completely. The healing of my scrape became my great teacher.

I understood that God's healing often took time. He would heal the places where I was ready to be healed. Often it wasn't in an instant, but since all healing is a miracle, I was satisfied to wait on God's timing (there was really no other choice). I felt as if I was always asking God to forgive me for the same things, and I tried. But now I had both a physical injury and the wound of unforgiveness that needed God's healing touch. What I failed to see was that God's healing was happening in both situations. It was incremental, not instant. The slow healing kept me focused on God. I couldn't heal myself physically or emotionally. Have you ever noticed that little wounds or even a tiny splinter can be painful and even debilitating? The slow healing process kept me aware of my pain and more aware of God. If I had had an instant healing, I might have said thank you and gone on my merry way and missed the miracle of forgiveness.

~~~~~~

I love beautiful flowers. Gardens are at their best when they are maintained. We have a plant in my garden called Virginia creeper, a tenacious weed that wraps itself around the stems of my flowers. If we don't get rid of it when it is small, it can destroy all the flowers as it winds its way through the entire garden. When I am attentive to my garden, I pull the weeds when they are very small. A garden truth: *small weeds have small roots.* They are much easier to pull when they are small. Unattended weeds may grow roots deep and wide in the garden or in our lives. Sooner is better than later.

When I can, I want to be rid of the issues, the unforgiveness, and the struggles that prevent me from a vibrant walk with God. In His perfect time, God shows me my trouble spots—gossip, jealousy, stretching the truth, and a hard heart. When God shows me these weeds, I know they need to go. Fortunately, they usually come to my attention one at a time. When I see them, I know that now is the time to ask for forgiveness, face the sin problem, and move on with my life and the Lord.

~~~~~~~

Back to where we started this chapter: "You crown the year with a bountiful harvest; even the hard pathways overflow with abundance" (Psalm 65:11).

There is a surprising truth and great hope in these words. This psalm assures us that even hard times can produce a harvest in our lives. In every difficulty, He can bless us with His abundant love and provision.

In the Rocky Mountains, most plants don't grow above the timberline. Recently, while hiking at 11,500 feet, I saw something surprising—several beautiful columbines were sprouting out of the rocks, where nothing else was growing.

I saw this as a picture of the "hard path that overflows with abundance."

There is never a place or a challenge we will face alone, without the resources of God Almighty. The rocks and the columbines reminded me of life. The rocks all around the columbines were hard, and like us, the flowers were delicate, almost fragile. In the middle of the rocks and hard ground, they were in full bloom, reproducing seeds and new flowers. I sensed that God was telling me not to be frightened by the challenges or the rocks that surround me, but to focus on living a productive and fruitful life even in the middle of difficulties. *Trust God!*

This is exactly what I learned from my parents: Trust God in the middle of every challenge and heartache. He knows all about it.

We will all experience difficult paths. Some are short and others may last a lifetime. On the dark path, we can be encouraged that God walks ahead of us, He sees the trials we will face, and He promises to be with us.

Often when we are on the difficult path, we are more willing to ask for and listen to the guidance of God. He is faithful and will not abandon us; He is all-loving and all-knowing. Throughout Scripture He promises His help. "Then call on me when you are in trouble, and I will rescue you" (Psalm 51:15). Never will we be alone on a difficult path. At the loneliest, lowest, most desperate place, we can't forget that God is always with us.

As I walk with God and trust Him, I have seen the abundant blessings on the hard paths. These blessings have been the peace that passes all understanding, the strength to stand and wait when I am in a spiritual battle, the ability to love and pray for people I might not like, and the freedom of being forgiven and forgiving others. Through these challenges and others, the truth of God's help in hard places becomes more real. We experience the power of Christ when we walk the hard path.

Because of the story of my sister's death, many have come to believe in Jesus. Women have lined up to have my mother counsel them and help them walk through forgiveness with their own painful situations. They realize that if she can forgive the one who killed her daughter, they can forgive their parent, husband, sibling, or friend. For more than fifty years, my mother has been a walking testimony, offering women fresh hope and a new perspective.

Laura's death taught me that God is the God of the resurrection. He brings new and fresh life from death. He will use everything in our lives to help us grow and live productive lives. When it comes to God, nothing is wasted, even our hurt and our pain. I have also learned that there is nothing I have experienced that is so painful or deep that God can't use it to strengthen me. Many of these answers and insights come after I have prayed, struggled, and released them to God.

Prayer is the beginning and the end of the difficult path. It helps us to trust God with our hard paths. Throughout history, we see people on difficult paths call out to God and watch as He supplies them with what they need for their journeys.

So much of what we do when we pray is asking God for our needs. In the next chapter, we will learn the power of the words *Ask God*.

Chapter 4

~~~

Prayers for the Path: Ask God

Ask me and I will tell you remarkable secrets
you do not know about things to come.
—*Jeremiah 33:3*

As I study the Bible, I am impressed by how often Jesus and others encourage us to ask.

God told the prophet Jeremiah to ask Him, and in return, He would show Jeremiah incredible secrets. Can we imagine what kind of secrets God might share with us? James wrote, "Yet you don't have what you want because you don't ask God for it" (4:2). What I love about James is how direct he was. James didn't beat around the bush; he broke things down and made them very clear: you don't have because you don't ask God.

One of the most inspiring stories in American history describing the power of asking God is the story of George Washington Carver. He transformed the economy of the South after the Civil War through prayer and the discovery of the mysteries of the peanut.

George was born in Missouri to a slave girl named Mary, owned by Moses and Susan Carver, German Americans. The young mother disappeared, and the Carvers raised young George as their own child after slavery was abolished. He was educated and eventually graduated from the University of Iowa in 1894, received his master's degree, and became the first black professor at Iowa State.

> The story is told that George Washington Carver had a sincere desire to help southern farmers rebound from the ravages of the Civil War and years of the soil being depleted by the planting of cotton. He couldn't get away from the idea that the answer could be found in peanuts and sweet potatoes. Being a godly man, he prayed that God would reveal to him the secrets of the universe. He told his friends that God replied, "Little man, you're too small to grasp the secrets of the universe. But I will show you the secret of the peanut." His research at the Tuskegee Institute resulted in the creation of more than three hundred products from peanuts—products like cooking oil, paint and, yes, peanut butter.[1]

A brilliant man with a simple faith revolutionized the American South. I wonder if there is even one person in the United States who has not been impacted by his discoveries? And to think it all began because he *asked* God to show him the secrets of the universe, and God responded with the secret of the peanut.

George Washington Carver's story inspires me and raises the questions, *What am I missing because I am not asking about the mysteries of God? Are there things God wants to tell me or show me? What are God's priorities for me?* I want to be like George Washington Carver, constantly asking God to show me, teach me, and help me understand. Prayer is the best place for us to learn and begin to ask.

Like Jeremiah, we are being challenged to ask God. Throughout the Bible, He commands us to ask, and He promises to respond. The following collection of scriptures encourages me to ask the Lord.

Ask me and I will tell you remarkable secrets you do not know about things to come. (Jeremiah 33:3)

> Ask me,
> > and I will make the nations your inheritance,
> > the ends of the earth your possession. (Psalm
> > 2:8 NIV)

You didn't choose me. I chose you. I appointed you to go and produce lasting fruit, so that the Father will give you whatever you ask for, using my name. (John 15:16)

You haven't done this before. Ask, using my name, and you will receive, and you will have abundant joy. (John 16:24)

You do not have because you do not ask God. (James 4:2 NIV)

Jesus used the Sermon on the Mount to lay out many of the Lord's priorities, including what our priorities in prayer should be. "Seek first His kingdom and His righteousness, and all these things will be added to you" (Matthew 6:33 NASB) is followed by one of the most dynamic teachings in Matthew:

> **A**sk and it will be given to you;
> **S**eek and you will find;
> **K**nock and the door will be opened to you. (7:7)

Ask. Seek. Knock. One of the most interesting discoveries I've made while writing this book has been to find that the very words Jesus used to teach us about asking spell the word *ASK*.

Repeatedly, God tells us to ask Him. Recently, this has become more important in how I live my life.

Because of the disciples' experiences, I am encouraged to ask the Lord for several things. I ask Him to help me understand His Word. Sometimes I read it but don't pay any attention to what I just read. I ask God to help me pay attention and remember what I am reading.

I ask for wisdom and discernment in my daily life, questions such as, *Where is God leading me? Is this situation a distraction, a disappointment, a discouragement, or an opportunity?*

The disciples asked Jesus several things. One of the most important was, "Lord, teach us to pray" (Luke 11:1 NIV), and Jesus responded with the most beloved prayer in all history, the Lord's Prayer. From time to time, I ask God to teach me how to pray. When you have prayed for as many years as I have, sometimes it's easy to become too familiar, too comfortable with prayer, and to forget to appreciate the power of prayer.

If Jesus' disciples, the men who devoted their lives to walking, following, and serving Jesus, needed to be taught to pray, then how much more do I need to learn?

Like the disciples, we can ask, "Lord, teach me to pray."

- As a mother, I ask for wisdom, knowledge, and understanding in guiding and encouraging my children.
- As a wife, I ask the Lord to show me how to love Tim in new ways and to give me patience and joy.
- As a daughter, I ask for compassion and peace as our parents age. I ask that the Lord would fill our parents with His strength and joy.
- As a grandmother, I ask the Lord to show me how to love our grandchildren and how to help guide them to become God-fearing adults.
- As a friend, I ask the Lord to show me how to love my friends and support them in their walk with the Lord. I ask how to be the friend my friends need.

- As a woman, I ask the Lord to fill me with the peace that passes all understanding, to help me be patient, kind, and caring. I ask that I would have the mind of Christ, to know and follow Him with wisdom. I also ask God to teach me how to love people with His love.

Another tool for prayers on the path is to pray the words the people of the Bible prayed.

One excuse people give is that they simply don't know what to pray. All a person needs to do is open the Bible and discover a collection of stories about the people of God and His work in and through their lives. It is full of a wide variety of prayers.

There are so many ways people ask God to direct their paths.

A great place to start is the book of Psalms. King David wrote some of my favorite prayers. They are succinct and filled with power:

> Teach me how to live, O Lord.
>   Lead me along the right path. (Psalm 27:11)

> Lead me in the right path, O Lord,
>   or my enemies will conquer me.
> Make your way plain for me to follow. (Psalm 5:8)

> Show me the right path. (Psalm 25:4)

> Make [my enemies'] path dark and slippery. (Psalm 35:6)

> Make me walk along the path of your commands,
>   for that is where my happiness is found. (Psalm 119:35)

> Point out anything in me that offends you,
> and lead me along the path of everlasting life.
> (Psalm 139:24)

This is one of the most important lessons on the path of life: pay attention and pray the words you find in the Bible.

From the examples above, we can see that God's people had great confidence and intimacy in their relationship with the Lord. Sometimes they were inquisitive, other times desperate, and always they asked for God's presence. Even though these words are thousands of years old, I am encouraged when I read them because they are so similar to the way people pray today.

Growing up in the Episcopal Church, I was raised reading the Book of Common Prayer. The prayers almost put me to sleep as a child, but as an adult, I realize that not only were they beautifully written; they were all based on Scripture.

One of my favorites is used at the conclusion of baptism, and is found on page 308 of the Book of Common Prayer:

> Heavenly Father, we thank you that by water and the Holy Spirit you have bestowed upon *these* your *servants* the forgiveness of sin, and have raised *them* to the new life of grace. Sustain *them*, O Lord, in your Holy Spirit. Give *them* an inquiring and discerning heart, the courage to will and to persevere, a spirit to know and to love you, and the gift of joy and wonder in all your works. *Amen.*[2]

This prayer is a collaboration of great prayers and promises. It includes many important ASKs directly from the prayers and stories of the Bible:

Sustain them, in your Holy Spirit: "For forty years you sustained them in the wilderness." (Nehemiah 9:21)

Give them an inquiring and discerning heart: "I will do what you have asked. I will give you a wise and discerning heart." (1 Kings 3:12 NIV)

Courage to will and to persevere: "Be strong and courageous! Do not be afraid or discouraged. For the LORD your God is with you wherever you go." (Joshua 1:9)

A spirit to know and to love you: "I am in them and you are in me. May they experience such perfect unity that the world will know that you sent me and that you love them as much as you love me." (John 17:23)

Through the years, these have become "word art," painting the most beautiful pictures that describe people's deep need for the Lord. Beyond praying Scripture and asking God, there are times just to ask for what you need. Nothing too spiritual or fluffy, simply honest prayer requests.

I have a favorite story that demonstrates the presence of God moving in our lives. Our (Tim's and my) family was growing and getting busier. Our happy house was situated between the bottom side of a blind hill and the edge of an inlet. We had one very strange feature in our new house. Two of the three doors on the backside opened out to the air. No deck, no ground, just two doors, suspended eight feet above the ground, begging for something to be built so we could walk out on it. The other door opened out to a small terrace. The dream was to build a large deck that would extend the length of the house so that every door could open out onto the deck.

The day arrived for the builder to begin the work and get the final plan for the deck that he would start the next day. The problem was that we hadn't finalized our decision, and Tim had left for China. The builder needed an answer, and I had to take the step.

What do we do? Spend the money or save it? The only thing I knew to do was to pray and ask the Lord.

Lord, I need You to show me: Do we build the deck or not? I nervously waited and hoped for an answer. God is so faithful and always full of surprises, and this was no exception. The response came quickly.

My Bible was open on the kitchen table to what happened to be the passage for the day: "Enlarge your house; build an addition. Spread out your home, and spare no expense!" (Isaiah 54:2). That was the perfect Scripture word picture for me!

Delighted, shocked, and thankful, I felt confident that God had given me the answer for our next step. What are the chances that the first time in my life I had ever prayed about an addition, the reading of the day specifically states, "Enlarge your house"? This is another time that God provided a surprising answer to my prayer. I am not really sure I had expected an answer at all.

The builder came to the house ready to go, and I told him about the prayer and what I had just finished reading. Confidently, I told him to build a deck and railing that would extend the length of the house. Isn't that what "enlarge your house" means? The deck became everyone's favorite place to play. Children rode tricycles and little pedal cars on it all day long. The children were close, penned in, and safe from the street and the water. God answered my weak prayer in a very strong and memorable way, and all I could do was say, "Thanks be to God for this indescribable gift."

We had no idea how important the deck would be to family happiness and safety. My friends called the deck "Lisa's playpen." And they were happy to bring their little ones over to the playpen, sip coffee together, and watch the pedal cars go back and forth. The new addition was needed, and it became especially important when we welcomed Abby, our fifth child. Once again we learned that God's promises are still important as we searched for and walked along God's path for our family. The words from Jeremiah 33:3 are powerful. God tells us to ask Him, and when we ask, we become more tuned in to God's presence and plans. When we ask, we are more alert and watching Him move and lead us through each day.

We are told to ask, but sometimes I wonder if I "over-pray," asking about too many personal and seemingly trivial things. Sometimes I wonder if I am burdening God or wasting His time. I see the Lord as my heavenly Father, and I want to ask Him about everything that helps me become more aware of God. Over the years, I've met with women who don't want to burden God with their prayers. They believe He is too busy and important to be bothered by their requests.

On the contrary, God is infinite, and our prayers do not deplete God's resources in any way. The Bible tells us that He has more than enough of everything. "For all the animals of the forest are mine, and I own the cattle on a thousand hills" (Psalm 50:10).

If I pray for wisdom for our family, or even an idea of what to fix for dinner, it doesn't mean if He answers my prayers, He doesn't have the resources to answer the prayers of a woman praying for her child in Brazil.

I love how Paul broke it down: "Always be joyful. Never stop praying. Be thankful in all circumstances, for this is God's will for you who belong to Christ Jesus" (1 Thessalonians 5:16–17).

Look at the words Paul just used: *always, never, in all circumstances.* Each one is a specific instruction to help us establish our priorities for success in our faith.

Paul gave another specific instruction: "Pray about everything."

Not just some things, not just the really important things, but all things. When it comes to talking to and asking God, Philippians 4 provides so much wisdom concerning how to pray, what to pray, and what happens when we pray: "Don't worry about anything; instead, pray about everything. Tell God what you need, and thank him for all he has done. Then you will experience God's peace, which exceeds anything we can understand. His peace will guard your hearts and minds as you live in Christ Jesus" (vv. 6–7).

I love the way the Bible clearly outlines how to live and what to do. Philippians 4:6–7 is a perfect guidebook for prayer:

- **Don't worry.** This is not a suggestion, but a command. Worry is unhelpful, unhealthy, and unproductive. Why waste our time and energy on worry? Nothing constructive happens when we worry.
- **Pray about everything.** Everything means *every* thing! We don't need to be afraid to pour our hearts out to God and tell Him what's on our minds. When it comes to prayer, there is nothing too big or too small.
- **Tell God what you need.** When we pray, we need to be specific. How will we know if and how God answers prayer if we aren't specific? God loves to have us come to Him about our lives and the things that concern us. When it comes to praying specifically, a prayer journal is a great way to document and write down our requests and concerns. The other blessing that comes when we write down our prayers is that we can point back to our specific requests and see how God answered them.
- **Thank Him for all He has done.** Even before we see the results we're looking for, we need to come into prayer with grateful, thankful hearts. When we choose to approach prayer

with a deep sense of gratitude for who God is, what He has done, and what He will do, our burdens are lifted, and we're reminded of God's truth and His power.

- **Experience God's peace.** This peace isn't like relaxing at the beach; we all understand that peace. Rather, the peace that passes all understanding is the kind of peace where we feel secure, loved, and safe when our world is falling apart everywhere else. This is the peace that comes when all hell breaks loose but we remain confident that God is with us in the chaos. This peace is a mystery, doesn't make sense, and is a miraculous gift from God. And it is a peace that protects us! How do we understand that kind of peace? By recognizing it is a gift from God. Like a miracle. We know that God is with us and He is in control. Our problems are not a surprise to Him, and there is nothing we will ever face that is greater than the power of God.

When you know the peace that passes all understanding, it will guard your heart and your mind as you live in Christ Jesus. "To guard" is best understood to be like a soldier, alert, guarding your heart and mind to protect it and keep it secure. By worrying less and praying about everything, our thoughts change, and so do our attitudes. We also become more aware of where God is in the details of our lives.

Often when it comes to prayer, we overthink or overanalyze our prayers, which is why I love the simplicity of Paul's instructions:

- Don't worry.
- Pray about everything.
- Tell God what you need.
- Thank Him for what He has done.

This passage is like a math problem:

Don't worry + pray + tell God + be thankful =
hearts and minds protected by God's peace

Our relationship with God will grow and mature as we practice and develop it. As we ask, we will seek, knock, and discover more. The promise is that our hearts and minds will be protected and guarded by God.

Chapter 5

~~~

The Parenting Path: Getting Started

Direct your children onto the right path,
and when they are older, they will not leave it.
—*Proverbs 22:6*

Trust in the LORD with all your heart;
do not depend on your own understanding.
Seek his will in all you do,
and he will show you which path to take.
—*Proverbs 3:5–6*

So follow the steps of the good,
and stay on the paths of the righteous.
—*Proverbs 2:20*

Parenting will improve your prayer life.
—*Babby Nelson, my wise mother*

The parenting path is the path of my life on which I have discovered the most about the unconditional, patient, and extravagant
love of God. I have also learned the most about my failures and

inadequacies, yet this is the path that has brought me the greatest joy, frustration, fear, satisfaction, and insight into the Lord's love for us. He is our Father, who loves us more than anyone could ever love us and knows us better than anyone will ever know us.

As a little girl, I hoped that one day I would be a mother. Caring for younger siblings and babysitting confirmed this desire. However, after the delivery of our first child, Laura, my thought when I was finally alone in my quiet hospital room was, *I hope we like her. I will never have another baby.* For the record, I had a *long* few days of labor and delivery, only to have a cesarean birth. Combine that with the hormones, and you can understand where I was coming from.

Thankfully, we did like her. In fact, we absolutely loved everything about Laura. To us, she was and still is our perfect child. She even slept through the night in the hospital. No babies do that! As she grew, her sweet and cooperative personality gave us the assurance that we were God's gift to perfect parenting. Remember the verse in Proverbs, "Pride goes before the fall"? We were humbled by our next child.

With our parental confidence in tow, we couldn't wait to have another baby. Two years after Laura, Elizabeth was born. Her arrival was a completely different experience. After a comparatively short labor, Elizabeth arrived with a head full of red hair and let out a mighty shout to let everyone know she had entered this world. I could tell instantly that this was going to be a different kind of adventure.

Elizabeth didn't sleep through the night until she was at least three and a half. She was determined, demanding, and she had a mind of her own. I told my mother that Elizabeth was my challenge and called her a brat. Mom's response to my comment was swift and definitive: "What you say is what you get. You can't talk about her like that."

My mother taught me never to label a difficult child. If the children heard me call them brats, she believed they felt more entitled to act like ones. When I would tell my friends my child was silly, she would become sillier. Called a yeller, she would yell more. The list is unending. And the opposite is true as well.

"My child is the best table setter." The child often wanted to show me that I was right.

"No one can make a bed like Willis does." We would watch him work on his bed. He took his success very seriously and loved it.

When I began to use positive words, my children sensed my confidence in them, and they often tried to live up to my expectations. For better or worse, I learned to watch the words I spoke to the children, over them, and about them. Like dynamite, words are explosive; they are more powerful than we know. What we think, speak, and declare can quickly become our reality. Calling your children brats, or worse, might negatively define them for life.

Instead of naming what I saw as "spoiled, bossy, difficult, and bratty," I changed my words to "determined, knows what she wants, a leader." Both sets of words were accurate, true, and powerful. But when Elizabeth heard them spoken about her, she began to see herself as a determined instead of a challenging child, a leader instead of a bully.

As I started to describe her with new positive words, I also grew to appreciate her strengths. Her strong qualities and personality became a gift and not as much of a challenge. By changing my descriptive words, I felt more positive toward her and spoke about her positively with my friends. They may have laughed at me because they knew I had a child with a full personality, but even they reacted differently to my "determined child" than to my "bratty child."

This is one of the most important, simple, and powerful lessons for the parenting path.

I would like to add that after what feels like more than one thousand parent-teacher conferences, I learned how important it is to listen to the teacher's observations but not to volunteer too much negative information about your child. In those conferences I learned that I had the opportunity to change the words a teacher might use to describe my child. Words like *talkative* and *doesn't listen* could become *inquisitive, communicative, confident,* and *thoughtful.*

People have accused me of being a Pollyanna, and there is some truth to that, but a positive mind-set and confidence in God as a partner with my parenting has enabled me to know that, at all times, God knows the strengths and weaknesses of my children and He has everything under control, even if I do not.

As the the children grew older, I focused on their differences and I made the mistake of taking the blame *and* the credit for their behavior. What I zeroed in on the most were the ways I felt I was *failing.* Why was one so energetic and strong-willed and the other so calm? I wanted them to be exactly the same, and I couldn't make it happen.

I didn't realize at the time that God had given us a gift of two children with very different personalities. Laura—easy, delightful, and an almost "perfect" child. Elizabeth—adventurous, determined, and brave. They were a perfect sibling combination.

Laura was a quiet leader. Elizabeth was a challenge to both Laura and us, but together, they were perfect. Laura could watch Elizabeth and help rein her in and give her guidance. Elizabeth challenged Laura to try new things. This has been a dynamic combination and has served them well for years. Today both are adventurous leaders and exhausted mothers of young children.

One danger of struggling with a child who has a mind of her own is that the word *failure* was a constant. If I told her not to step over the line, she would step on top of it. With a sparkle in her eyes and her foot on the line, but not over it, she knew she had totally outsmarted me. She was on the line, not over the line! I could discipline for disobedience but not for being outsmarted.

I would overreact with anger and harsh words as I attempted

64

to get her to do what I needed her to do. The more she refused, the louder I spoke. Harsh, frustrated, angry words erupted from this worn-out mother who constantly felt like the biggest failure. Putting her to bed was a battle, and making her stay there was even worse. I couldn't get her into her car seat without her arching her back, crying, and fighting me. Laura would just climb into hers.

I prayed and struggled to think of ways to succeed. Occasionally God would assure me in His own way that He was still with me. A thought, a word came to me saying, *Do you remember being pregnant with your children? Do you remember how peaceful Laura was in utero and how incredibly active Elizabeth was? I created these children. They are very different and both are wonderful. Ask Me for all that you need and I will guide you. Do the best you can, and don't take the credit or the blame. They are My children and I am their heavenly Father.*

This was an earthshaking truth. They were *created* to be different. Before I could even hold them in my arms, God was creating them to be Laura and Elizabeth. Their personalities were beyond my control from their initial creation.

HWJP (How Would Jesus Parent?)

One of my most memorable nights, I was lying awake, agonizing over my failures as a mother. In my sleepy mind, I believed I was ruining all three of my children. Willis, the baby, was just getting started in life, and I felt that he was already ruined. Poor boy didn't have a chance. I don't think I was asking God anything, but I may have prayed one of my favorite prayers: "I don't know what to do! But my eyes are on you" (2 Chronicles 20:12). The Robertson translation: "Help me! I'm desperate, and I'm looking to You for help."

I knew the words of Jeremiah 33:3, "Ask me and I will show you great and mighty things which you do not know" (paraphrased), but did they apply to motherhood?

After praying my desperate prayer, a very clear thought came to my heart: *Your discipline is driving Elizabeth away. Don't be her Marine Corps drill sergeant and make demands of her. Put your arm around her and be her coach. Encourage her and guide her where you want her to go.*

Truth resonated in those words, and they completely changed my life and my method of mothering. When I was a child, my mother was like a Marine Corps drill sergeant. Imitating her was the only way I knew how to mother. Be stern, strict, and show them who is the boss. And now I was discovering that God was showing me a better way—His way for me to be a mother.

I hardly slept that night and couldn't wait for Elizabeth to get up so I could put my arm around her. The most life-changing part wasn't just that God gave me wisdom to raise Elizabeth, but in that moment, I realized that God cared about *me* and about our children. He wanted me to ask Him, and most important, I knew that if I partnered with Him, together we would succeed.

And we did succeed as I learned to listen and follow the guidance of the Holy Spirit. The Lord wanted to show me the best ways to parent in each specific parenting challenge.

Through this and other experiences, I learned that as parents we are to be imitators of Christ. This question gnawed in my mind. Before WWJD (What Would Jesus Do?) became popular, I was thinking about HWJP: How Would Jesus Parent?

If God is my heavenly Father, how does He parent me? Is He a bully to His children? Is He harsh, rude, or cruel? Does He taunt or torment them? Does He ridicule His children? Does He make promises and not keep them? Can I trust Him?

When I thought about the ways God parents me, His child, I

could figure out the better way to parent our children. As my own children did to me, I did to the Lord. I disobeyed, said things I shouldn't, lied, rebelled, had a hard heart, and more. I needed to be their mother, teacher, leader, and coach. When necessary, they needed wise and effective discipline.

How I struggled with discipline! My method was to reach into a drawer for my wooden spoon and smack it loudly and threateningly on my open hand. I don't know that I ever used it, but the spoon scared the children and it scared me.

On one desperate day, this question challenged me: *Is this how God disciplines me?*

It stunned my anger. I knew the answer was a resounding *no*.

I began to think about how God disciplines me, His child. Had the Lord ever yelled at me in utter frustration? Ugly confession, I have yelled at a child so passionately that I strained my vocal cords. It was painful and took a few days to heal. I wondered if God was punishing me because I had lost control of myself. Can you imagine God chasing His child with a wooden spoon in His hand? I am ashamed of myself and embarrassed too.

I knew these were ridiculous thoughts, but God's ways are higher than our ways. His thoughts are higher than our thoughts. In the area of discipline, I needed some new ideas.

A simple but effective discipline had to do with my children saying bathroom words, or "potty talk." You can be sure that with five energetic children and their friends, potty talk could be a problem. The first time or two inappropriate words were spoken, I washed their mouths out with soap because that's what my mother always threatened to do. And then I had a better idea. I told the children they could say whatever they wanted to say, but potty talk was only for the bathroom and they had to be by themselves. Entertaining yourself with bad words isn't fun when you are alone in the bathroom and no one can hear you.

As the children grew, my prayers changed. Sometimes I would pray, *Lord, they are Your little children—You know how they are made and how they work. To me they are all like cuckoo clocks. I don't understand them. Please show me what makes them tick and how I can get them to do what they need to do.*

One of our most important goals as parents was to introduce our children to Christ and help them walk their own walk with Jesus. For some children this was easy; they believed what we said and wanted what we offered them. But I had one little girl who wasn't so sure about Jesus.

We worked hard to give our children the best Christian foundation. Church every Sunday, family devotions, talking about prayers and answers to prayers during car rides. Our expectation was that when we were ready, they would accept Christ as their Lord and Savior. Notice that I said "when we were ready." We never thought about when they might be ready. They went to Christian preschools and had Christian friends, family, and books. They heard Bible stories, were prayed for in the womb, and more. How could they resist the invitation of Jesus?

Little Cally was our holdout for a short while. With all of our Christian community being poured into her life, she wasn't so sure Jesus was for her. In her school, the children were always invited to make a commitment to Christ, and she never took the teacher up on the offer. We and her teacher were alarmed that she didn't jump at this wonderful invitation. When asked if she had Jesus in her heart, she would matter-of-factly say no.

Cally was my fourth child. All the others had been so willing and eager to have Jesus in their hearts, but she was different. She was still so young but also very resistant. We continued to lead our family in the way of the Lord and prayed for this stubborn little heart.

I will never forget bedtime conversation with her. I had read her an inspiring Bible story, prayed a great prayer, and asked her, "Cally, would you like to ask Jesus to come into your heart?"

Her answer was a simple no. No reasons, no details; she simply didn't want to.

We continued to pray and wait.

One day, as we were driving in a shopping center parking lot, in her usual understated way, Cally gave me the good news.

"Mom, if you want Jesus in your heart, all you have to do is ask Him, right?"

I nodded and wondered where this was going.

She continued, "Last night, in bed, I asked Jesus to come into my heart, and He said He would. And He did."

This was not at all what I was expecting, but it worked for her and it worked for me!

Stopping at the grocery store before heading home, I bought a turkey breast, cranberries, and mashed potatoes. Our spring dinner turned into a Thanksgiving meal. From that day forward, we have had a Thanksgiving dinner whenever we are especially thankful for something. Why should we save the turkey and cranberries only for November?

The most amazing part of this story is that Cally changed after she invited Jesus into her heart. She became kinder, more patient, helpful, and generous. Adults are expected to change, but never had I expected a child to change when she prayed the sinner's prayer. Christ touched her life and began shaping her into His servant.

A Cautionary Prayer

As the children grew, we had another family favorite prayer. Warning: don't pray this unless you mean it.

Lord, You are with my children right now. You know who they are with and what they are doing. If they are doing anything that will get them into trouble now or even later in life, please let them be caught.

I would pray this for the children and often with the children. They hated it. Yes, they did get caught. A little stealing or a little cheating brought some to the attention of their teachers. Fortunately for them and for us, they were still young and the ones who caught them made certain they learned some good life lessons.

One child wept as she told me, "That isn't fair. You always pray that we will be caught and we do get caught. None of my friends do. It isn't fair!"

Once while teaching a MOPS (Mothers of Preschoolers) group, I shared this powerful prayer. Several weeks later a father came to me and told me that his teenage son had been kicked out of school for stealing. His crushing comment was, "My wife blames *you* for this. She prayed that if our children were doing anything wrong, they would be caught. Well, thanks to you, he was caught and expelled. Thanks a lot!" They left the church shortly after that.

That wasn't exactly how I wanted this to turn out. However, my firm belief for our family was that it was better for our children to get caught by us or by the school when they were young and teachable than to let them get really good at lying, cheating, and attending or planning wild parties. As they grew up, the stakes—the cost of being caught—would be much higher.

~~~~~~

As the leader of a women's Bible study for many years, I had the privilege of praying for and with many mothers as they struggled with raising their children. Few got through the teenage years without fears or tears. We all worried and prayed together. The prayers for our children unified us for years and maybe even a lifetime. Have I mentioned that parenting improves our prayer life?

I will always remember one mother's prayers in particular. Cathy was the mother of four of the most beautiful and seemingly perfect children. The Lentz family Christmas card was always a family favorite of ours. They all looked so happy with their beautiful smiles, and our children thought they looked like a Colgate toothpaste commercial.

What's more important is that the family's inner beauty matched their outward attractiveness. They radiated God's love and joy—their passion for Jesus and His power was infectious. Cathy was the picture of wisdom and faith for many of us as we struggled to learn how to succeed as parents.

Similar to our family, they had three daughters and one son—we have four daughters and a son. Their children were a little older than mine, and they made the perfect babysitters for my family. We often got two or three babysitters for the price of one, which is a major benefit when you're talking about five children!

Willis loved it when their son, Carl, would accompany his sisters to our house. Carl was athletic and fun, and he understood what it meant to be the only boy in a family surrounded by busy girls. He taught Willis some tricks for his sisters, and they always had a good time. The girls loved it, too, when Carl came. What's not to love about a good-looking older boy showing up at their house on a Saturday night? We affectionately called him Prince Charming.

Like most seemingly perfect Christian families, as their children grew older, there were seasons of wandering. Even with his God-loving parents, growing up in a home surrounded by God's truth, Carl wasn't always the perfect "church boy." His taste in music drove his parents crazy. Cathy and Steve carefully watched, prayed, and loved him. And for a short while, Carl went his own way.

Steve told me about a time he drove his son's car and checked out his music collection. As Steve drove down the road, he tossed every CD out the window that had inappropriate lyrics. That was a very expensive car ride.

As Carl's parents struggled, those who watched learned from them. Some disciplines worked well; others were not successful. Cathy remembers a moment that changed her. Steve and Carl were talking near the garage. Steve told teenage Carl that if he moved out of their house, he could make his own decisions, but as long as he lived with them, he would abide by their rules. Going to church every Sunday was one of the nonnegotiable rules. This was so hard for all of them.

Carl did move out for six weeks, and when he returned they sent him to Hargrave Military Academy. There was a price to be paid for Carl's bad decisions, and Carl paid it. The Lentz family strongly believed that when parents keep enabling their children, the result will be dependent children. Determined to work hard, raise independent children, and pray for their children, Steve and Cathy pressed on.

Cathy gave me some wise advice: "You don't know who you are raising! Don't be afraid to make the hard choices." They had no idea about the call of God on Carl's life. But they knew they had to do what they thought God was asking them to do.

Every child is a child of the King of kings and the Lord of all. They are gifts given to us by God, and we have the God-given responsibility to raise them well, knowing that one day we return them to God.

Children raised in Christian homes may wander away from the faith for a season. Sometimes when a child has been raised in a strong Christian family, their faith is their family's and not their own. No matter how strong the family is, there is a time when children need to have their own encounters with Jesus. They need the assurance that Jesus saved them (not their parents, but them), and they need to make their faith real and personal.

Once I explained it to Tim this way: I didn't grow up with an active faith embedded in the culture of my family. At night I lay awake, wondering about the meaning and purpose of life. I had a sense of a life with a "happily ever after," but I also wondered why we were on earth.

On the other hand, Tim grew up with a family who had a strong faith. He walked through life with a certainty about heaven, confident of God's love and purpose, never questioning the "whys" of life. In college, we both had encounters with God but experienced them in different ways. For the first time in my life, I had a radical encounter with Jesus, meeting Jesus in a real and powerful way.

When I discovered a relationship with Christ, the words of "Amazing Grace" leapt off the song sheet and into my heart. "I once was lost, but now am found, was blind but now I see." I had been lost, and now I was so appreciative to meet and know Jesus. After my first encounter with Him, I was an enthusiastic and grateful Christian. I lived the words *on fire for the Lord*. That was me! Jesus had saved me, changed my life, and I wanted everyone to know it.

When Tim encountered God in college, he was grateful and appreciative, but because he knew so much about the Lord, he had never felt lost. Overall, his personality is calmer than mine, and from a young age, he knew and had an assurance that God was always with him. Tim's question was whether he wanted to commit himself to the lifestyle that was required to serve God. Thankfully, he did.

Tim and Carl Lentz had this in common—a wonderful confidence about the Lord that was instilled in them at a young age by faithful, praying parents. Both of them knew the Lord, His love, His purpose in life. Yet each of them had a journey where they wandered away from Christ's best for a season. Because of the Lord's faithfulness, and their parents' prayers, they each returned to

Jesus. And when they did, they had gained a greater understanding and appreciation of God's redemption, love, and purpose for them.

Cathy was always an inspiration to me, a pillar of faith, even when the ground felt shaky. Whenever I asked her how Carl was doing, rather than throwing up her hands in frustration, criticizing Carl for his choices, or displaying anger toward God, she calmly and confidently would say, "Carl is working on his testimony." No panic, no fear, no hopelessness, just an inspiring confidence that God would use all things together for good! *And* He did! Not only was Carl radically transformed, but God put a call on his life for ministry.

Today Carl is the senior pastor of Hillsong Church New York. God has given him an international platform. Yes, Carl was working on his testimony, and God continues to use that testimony to share the gospel message of Jesus' saving, transforming grace to hundreds of thousands.

Cathy's words, "You never know who you are raising and who they will turn out to be," reminded me that every prayer we pray for our children is an investment, and not one prayer is wasted. They are powerful and a direct communication from your heart to the heart of God. Prayer is like a growing oak tree: we can plant the acorn, but only God can make it grow, and sometimes it takes a little time for a small acorn to grow into a big oak tree.

Never Give Up

We can rejoice, too, when we run into problems and trials, for we know that they help us develop endurance. And endurance develops strength of character, and character strengthens our confident hope of salvation. And this hope will not lead to disappointment. For we know how dearly God loves us, because he has given us the Holy Spirit to fill our hearts with his love. (Romans 5:3–5)

When it comes to parenting, here is my best advice: *never give up!* Yes, we will get discouraged, disappointed, and depressed by what we experience in our lives. But we must remember that in every situation, every tear, every fight, every bit of confusion and frustration, God is still with us.

God never wastes anything, and He will use all our circumstances to teach us. When we pray, we learn to depend on God's faithfulness, not ourselves. These prayers will give us hope. "And this hope will not lead to disappointment. For we know how dearly God loves us, because he has given us the Holy Spirit to fill our hearts with his love" (Romans 5:5).

To quote Thomas Edison, "Our greatest weakness lies in giving up. The most certain way to succeed is always to try just one more time."[1]

God, as our Father, never gives up on us, His children. We should never give up on Him.

Chapter 6

~~~

The Parenting Path: Letting Go

For he will order his angels
to protect you wherever you go.
They will hold you up with their hands
so you won't even hurt your foot on a stone.
—*Psalm 91:11–12*

Be still and know that God is God—their Father.
—*Psalm 46:10 (paraphrased)*

Our parenting evolves as our children age. When we hold our precious newborns for the first time, we need to realize that we are the best parents they have. They depend on us for most everything, and we are responsible for them and all they need. Most of our time and attention are consumed by our new babies.

Little by little children grow and become more independent. We couldn't send a newborn to kindergarten, and a five-year-old isn't ready for middle school or college. One of the miracles of parenting is that as we partner with God, He teaches us how to parent all ages and stages. And when they are ready to go to college, hopefully we are prepared and willing to release them to that world.

My mother often joked that I was so awful to her the summer before I left for college, and because of that, she couldn't wait for me to go, and I couldn't wait to leave. She believed that in the final summer months between high school and college, when we had so much conflict, God was preparing our hearts to separate from each other. Because we loved each other so much, we didn't want to separate, but our conflicts made it much easier for me to leave for college.

The Lord never stops parenting us, and as parents we need to help our children grow into the people He has designed them to be. Yes, I am still always learning new things about parenting. One of the most challenging lessons I learned as they were in their teens and heading into adulthood was the importance of releasing my children to the world and to the Lord. This was a hard one for me.

I have had a child or two whom I wanted to fully control, but only for a season. (They needed me and couldn't live without me! Or so I thought.) God had a tender way of helping me give each child to Him, learn to trust Him, trust the child, and let go.

We love our younger children in a different way than we do the older ones, and maybe that is God's design and plan. We aren't ready to leave them when they are young, but when they mature, it is time for them to fly.

The psalmist said we are fearfully and wonderfully made. I learned that God has a plan for each of our five children, and I needed to ask Him and trust Him for that plan.

Raising children isn't a secret; it is a partnership with God. He did show me great and wonderful things. Sometimes He showed me things that I didn't really want to know but nevertheless needed to know.

We were always mindful of the parenting advice from Proverbs:

Direct your children onto the right path,
>> and when they are older, they will not leave it. (22:6)

Trust in the LORD with all your heart;
>> do not depend on your own understanding.
Seek his will in all you do,
>> and he will show you which path to take. (3:5–6)

So follow the steps of the good,
>> and stay on the paths of the righteous. (2:20)

There were two important ways Tim and I applied these words to raising children.

First, we made a firm commitment that our family would always be in church every Sunday. Tim, raised Baptist, was used to this deep church loyalty; I was not as loyal to Sunday church attendance. However, for our family, going to church, Sunday school, and youth group were never optional. If our children spent the night out, we would pick them up for church; if friends were with us, they would go to church with us or their parents would pick them up.

We insisted that our children go to church. It was the best way we knew to raise Christian children. Tim knew that children needed to be taught about the Lord and that a relationship with Christ doesn't just happen. It was an effort for all of us. The promise and hope of this proverb is that if they are taught to know the Lord, when they are older, they will not leave this path.

I counted on God to guide us as we guided our children to follow Him.

Please know that our church wasn't perfect; there were long seasons when the Sunday school and church were mediocre at best, and our children came up with every excuse they could think of not to go: "All the wrong people go to youth group," "None of our friends go," "It is boring," "I have too much homework." You name it, we heard it. But because Sunday church was not negotiable while they lived in our house, eventually they all learned not to fight us about it because they wouldn't win. Of course, there were some extenuating circumstances, like sickness and travel, but not many.

I credit Tim's unwavering fortitude with the surprising success of our commitment to church. Even I wanted to stay home and take a break, but we never did. We honored God on Sundays and held Hebrews 10:25 close to us: "And let us not neglect our meeting together, as some people do, but encourage one another." To my surprise, this truth was filled with a lifetime of blessings for all of us.

Many times we would fight or argue all the way to church, park the car, put on our smiles, and go through the door in our anger and frustration. But God met us there and blessed us just for showing up, bad attitudes and all. One of the blessings of going to church is that I don't remember one time when we continued the fight or argument after church.

I need to add that one of the reasons for the success of this strategy was that we tried to make Sunday a happy day. Somehow we started the tradition of "Red Head Lagoon." Laura came up with the name for our special lunch after church. Some days we would pick up delicious deli sandwiches, Slurpees, or bagels. After church we would have a family celebration.

Some may think of this as bribery, but we think of it as positive reinforcement, and it worked for us.

As the children graduated from high school, each one continued going to church in his or her college years. They met lifetime friends, future bridesmaids, and Elizabeth and Cally married men they met in their college fellowship groups. Laura met her husband on a blind date at our church's women's retreat—yes, a women's retreat! Willis met his wife at church too. God works in mysterious ways! As the children grew up, the routine of Sunday with the Lord continued to be an important part of their week.

One reason that Proverbs 22:6, "Direct your children onto the right path, and when they are older, they will not leave it," is so loved by parents is that it ends with a promise for the parent and the child. Parents, or the adults in the child's life, lay the foundation for the child; if the child should stray from the path, the promise is that eventually they will return. My theory on why they return is because when they are away from the Lord, out of fellowship, they are no longer "feeding on the Bread of Life," or the Word of God.

Over the years, I have seen children and even some of my friends who have fed on the Lord and His Word become spiritually hungry when they are out of fellowship. They begin to miss the spiritual nourishment for their lives and they are starving, famished.

Nourishment is one of my favorite words. Jesus is described as the Bread of Life (John 6:35, 47–51 THE MESSAGE). We are told to "taste and see that the LORD is good" (Psalm 34:8). When we are active in our faith, we receive spiritual nourishment. Like physical food, spiritual food sustains us, satisfies us, fortifies us, and lets us enjoy the company and fellowship of others. Once you get used to the feeling of being nourished, you will learn when you are malnourished or undernourished.

The second principle we drew from Proverbs was to deliberately partner with God and ask Him to equip us as the parents to our specific children.

The words of these verses for parenting are straightforward and available to all. No wonder these are a few of the most powerful and popular verses for parents. Look at these specific words of instruction:

- Direct
- Guide

- Trust in the Lord
- Do not depend on your own understanding
- Seek God's will
- Look for the path to unfold
- Follow the steps of the good
- Stay *on the path!*

These are imperative words, almost commands, and they give us very specific guidance.

Parents are chosen by God for their children. God will equip us to lead them on the right path for them and teach us how to get there too. But we need to get going and follow it.

As God guided us, we learned how to guide and lead our children one step at a time.

Again, the success of this way of parenting was in our partnership with God. Think about the partnership this way: I love to dance with Tim. He loves music and he loves to dance. When the music begins, Tim will extend his hand to me and lead me to the dance floor. I follow him there. And when we hit the dance floor together, we are at our best when and if I follow his lead. I have to trust him. More than once, I have tried to take over the lead, and that always leads to confusion and sore toes. I want to lead Tim, but we dance the best when he leads me and I trust him. Sometimes I want to lead the Lord as I parent. But it always works best when I follow His lead.

This may be a simple illustration, but it helps me understand the concept of being in partnership with God. God invites us; we accept. God will lead us to great places if we follow Him. We can join the dance, the journey, the life, confident that God has the dance, a plan, a purpose, a song for us.

My mother's words rang in my heart again as I watched our children grow older: "Being in the center of God's will is the place of our greatest happiness. You will never be happier apart from God's plan than you will be following Him."

I might translate this to my children in this way: "Being in the arms of God as He swirls me around to the song of life is the place of my greatest joys, challenges, and great adventures. My greatest happiness is when I stay in the arms of God."

As parents we must pray, pay attention, and persevere with the Lord and our families. Never lose sight of the truth that God does the "heavy lifting," the hard work. God transforms lives; we can't do that for our children or ourselves. Understanding this truth leads us to once again surrender our children to the Lord and invite Him into this part of our lives. Here's a sample prayer you can pray:

Heavenly Father,

Thank You for this beautiful child. Thank You that You chose me to be [his or her] parent. Thank You that [she or he] is fearfully and wonderfully made. [He or she] belongs to You, and I have the privilege to be [his or her] mother. You know how [he or she] works; You understand exactly where [he or she] is. Please, Lord, guide all of us through this situation—[fill in the blank]—and help [him or her] know Your presence, protection, and power.

In Jesus' name, amen.

We may be able to be good parents on our own, but we found that God's insights led us on an excellent path, and with God working through us, we could be more effective parents. Our decision to partner with God enabled us to travel the parenting path with a little more confidence because we knew that God had gone before us, He was leading us, and He was giving us what we needed to succeed as parents.

We witnessed this firsthand with Elizabeth.

One of the joys and challenges of being a parent is trying to keep on top of helping your children do the right thing, even when they do the wrong thing.

One summer night, Elizabeth disobeyed us. Neither Tim nor I can remember what she did, but we do remember her discipline. The result was one of our better moments as parents. A consequence was deserved, and we wrestled with what it should be. To settle on the right discipline, we gave her a choice. She could be grounded for the rest of her life, or she had to try out for the varsity field hockey team. Every August, the team had a two-week tryout known as "Hell Week," with practice for three hours in the morning and two hours in the afternoon. The girls worked very hard the whole two weeks.

Elizabeth had played years of field hockey as a child, but she was probably not destined for a college scholarship. Dutifully, she went to every Hell Week practice, came home, and promptly fell asleep. Exhausted but relieved that she wasn't grounded for the rest of her life, she persevered. To no one's surprise, that year she didn't make the varsity team, but she did play on the junior varsity team and did well. Tim and I were always on the field, cheering the team to victories. The team fathers were soon named the "Bad Dads" because they often tried to coach from the stands or correct the referees. They were enthusiastic and faithful to their girls. Their daughters were appreciative and embarrassed.

What made this form of discipline so effective was that it enriched Elizabeth and didn't deplete her. The following year, Elizabeth did make the varsity team, and her senior year, she was a captain of the team. The discipline we gave Elizabeth evolved into something that fortified her. Field hockey ended up being a major part of her high school experience, and she eventually thanked us for our creative discipline. A discipline the child thanks you for? Now we're talking!

This is so memorable because this particular form of discipline added to her life and ours. We were all better because of it. So many of our attitudes about discipline were angry and limiting. Yes, it is right for discipline to be restrictive, but when the Lord disciplines us, it improves our lives. It doesn't set us back. We prayed that our discipline would add to our children's lives, not destroy their spirits.

Prayerful discipline became more important to us because we realized that God cares about how we discipline. He wants the discipline we use to benefit the children, the parents, and the family.

How does God discipline us? Well, "think about it" (Deuteronomy 8:5). The Bible tells us He does it "for our own good." To me that means that He plans our discipline for our ultimate good. He doesn't react in anger. Neither should we. So many teachings from the Bible on discipline educated us as we parented.

The book of Proverbs has many keys for successful parenting. For example, "The Lord disciplines those he loves, as a father the son he delights in" (3:12 niv).

We are disciplined by God because He loves us. The question for us is do we express our love through our discipline?

Solomon continued:

> My son, obey your father's commands,
>   and don't neglect your mother's instruction.
> Keep their words always in your heart.
>   Tie them around your neck.
> When you walk, their counsel will lead you.
>   When you sleep, they will protect you.
>   When you wake up, they will advise you.
> For their command is a lamp
>   and their instruction a light;
> their corrective discipline
>   is the way to life. (Proverbs 6:20–23)

Is our discipline constructive? Does it teach and enrich the child and the family?

"People who accept discipline are on the pathway to life, but those who ignore correction will go astray" (Proverbs 10:17). At times I have known that my children were misbehaving. Instead of addressing the issue, sometimes I would I turn my back and pretend I didn't see what they were doing. I was tired of dealing with their bad behavior. My lame thinking was that if I didn't see it, I didn't have to correct them. So I tried not to see it. Take it from me—this is not a good idea.

"Discipline your children while there is hope. Otherwise you will ruin their lives" (Proverbs 19:18). There is a season and a time for discipline. We need to pay attention to this and seize the right time for correction.

"Fathers, do not provoke your children to anger by the way you treat them. Rather, bring them up with the discipline and instruction that comes from the Lord" (Ephesians 6:4). What an important insight. I have thought about the result of my parents' discipline of me as a child and how I respond to God's discipline. To my parents' discipline, I would respond with rebellion, anger, and a hard heart. When they disciplined in anger, I responded with the same. The Lord's discipline to me is loving, and most of the time I respond with sorrow, but I hope to be teachable and learn from it. When we discipline with the wisdom of God, it will add to the child's life and to ours. It will build it, not tear it down.

"For God has not given us a spirit of fear and timidity, but of power, love, and self-discipline" (2 Timothy 1:7). This is one of my favorite verses. It applies more to parenting than to the disciplining of children. The power in these words is staggering on many levels. It begins by identifying a "spirit of fear." The verse defines what God has and has not given us. I have experienced a spirit of fear as a debilitating insecurity or torment and mental anguish. When I see these in my life or the lives of others, I am certain they are not godly, but quite the opposite. But according to this promise, God gives us power, love, and self-discipline, which is also translated as "a sound mind" in the New King James Version.

More than once I have prayed against the spirit of fear and proclaimed the gift of power, love, and a sound mind. This was powerful because I was claiming the words of Scripture and taking a stand against the lies and destruction of Satan.

To me these are some of the most important ingredients to successful Christian parenting:

- Imitate the Lord's ways of discipline. How would Jesus parent your child or you?
- Seek a partnership with God. Invite Him to guide and teach you as you lead your children.
- Be confident that the Lord wants you to succeed as parents and He cares that your children succeed too.
- Persevere with what you feel in your soul is the right thing to do. More than once the children talked me out of what I knew was right, but when we dared to stay strong on important issues (like field hockey tryouts) and implement God-inspired and wise discipline, it transformed our family.
- Surround your children with godly examples. The people caring for your children are among the most important ones to influence them. Prayerfully select them and let them know that their job with your children is their ministry, not just a job. They are working for you and the Lord.
- Discipline with prayer and thought. See it as an opportunity to strengthen the children and the family, not to demoralize or hurt them. Imitate God's ways in your life.

God cares about our success as parents. When we partner with Him, He will show us the best path for us and our families.

~~~~~~

As teenagers, our children were excited about the chance to go on mission trips. Yes, mission trips have so many great purposes, serving God and serving people, but another real draw was the opportunity for life-changing travel with a group of leaders and other children the parents trust.

Laura was the first one to leave us for a trip to Bolivia, and later she ventured to Namibia, South Africa, China, and other exotic places. Elizabeth felt called to Sri Lanka, the Dominican Republic, and Honduras; Willis went to Tanzania, Kazakhstan, Israel, and Thailand; Cally and Abby traveled to Thailand, China, the Dominican Republic, and more.

There was one awful night when every child was in a different part of the world: Abby was in the rice fields of China, Cally and Willis were in Thailand, Elizabeth was in Sri Lanka, and Laura was at the G8 Summit in Great Britain. I woke up frozen with fear for all of them and for me. Where exactly were they? What were they doing? Were they safe? Yes, I knew the organizations they were with, but I couldn't easily reach any one of them. Icy fear, the worst kind of fear, consumed me, and I felt totally helpless. I prayed, but it was more of a reaction to fear than a meaningful prayer. And of course, God was there.

I saw a picture in my mind of the whole world, and I zeroed in on the countries. Do you know the song "He's Got the Whole World in His Hands"? It played in my head that night and it comforted me.

God knew precisely where each child was, and He was with them. He had put His angels over them, to guard them in all of their ways (Psalm 91:11). I needed to be still and know that God is God, their Father (Psalm 46:10). He loves them more than I ever could. And He loves me too.

I also thought of 2 Chronicles 16:9: "The eyes of the LORD search the whole earth in order to strengthen those whose hearts are fully committed to him." This concept gave me great comfort because I knew that His eye was on each one, all at the same time. Worrying and fear weren't helping my children or me.

God could see Elizabeth being chased out of the jungles of Sri Lanka by Buddhist monks (thankfully I couldn't see that!). He could see Laura sliding down the sand dunes in Africa or at her job at the G8 Summit with Bono and George Clooney (she even got a peck on the cheek from George!). He could see Willis with a fisherman whose boat had been destroyed in the tsunami of Thailand. He could see Cally working with trafficked women in Thailand, establishing a company where they earned money by making leather purses. And He could see Abby working in the rice fields of western China. The pictures they sent were beautiful, but each one felt so far away and so independent!

God assured me that He knew where each child was and that He was there too. My best option was to trust and release each child to His care. The other option was to make myself crazy, consumed with fear, doubts, and worry.

You may wonder, "How could she let her children travel all over the world at such young ages?"

One Sunday morning in church, God gave me a picture, and it prepared me to let them go when the time came. He helped me learn how to take my worries and turn them into powerful prayers. A worried and scared mother can't help but pray with a desperate power. That Sunday I sat behind Claire, a close friend of my in-laws. I am a generation behind her, and her children are the generation between my children and me. I watched when Claire's children were in high school and she bravely let them travel the world on mission trips. I knew her children had been in Africa, China, and other places. She always appeared to be peaceful as she celebrated and delighted in their adventures.

In this picture, I saw Claire as a beautiful peach tree, full of sweet, ripe peaches. Like any healthy tree, when the fruit is ripe, the fruit will drop off the tree. Because I had been close to her, watching her parent her older children, her ripe peaches—her fruit of peace, confidence, and trust—planted in my garden, and I grew my own peach tree with the fruit of peace, confidence, and trust. A fruitful tree!

"Be fruitful and multiply," Genesis 1:22 and 28 tell us. Up until that day, I thought Genesis was talking only about populating the world, and since that day sitting behind Claire, I wonder if being fruitful might also mean reproducing the work of the Lord in our lives.

Claire's peace and joy as she raised her children were contagious. I wanted to imitate her and try to do the same with my family. Because I was close to her, or in her garden, I was benefiting from her fruit as a mother. Proverbs 2:20 tells us to "follow the steps of the good, and stay on the paths of the righteous." I admired Claire as a mother and followed her steps and her path. She helped me more than she will ever know as I allowed my children to grow and go.

I will never forget the struggle I had with Willis wanting to move to Los Angeles immediately after college. Our son, our little boy, was ready and excited to take on the world in LA, the other side of the country. If he had wanted to go for a season, that would have been easier. But he was moving, taking his car, finding a home, a job, and new friends. He was eager to be a man, and he was well on his way.

As Willis packed for his move, I helped him. My heart ached, but I kept it to myself. In my wrestling with God and my emotions,

I had a thought that totally changed my perspective on this change to our family: *Willis belongs to God.*

We had the privilege to raise him, but Willis belonged to God. What if Willis had announced after four years of college that he would never leave me, our home, and our family? What if he had told me that he wanted to work at the local Burger King forever and stay in his own room? This would have made me shriek and shoo him out the front door. I didn't mind Burger King; I just didn't want him living at home forever. As his parents, we raised our children to fly and be independent. I had to release my hold and let him fly, with my blessing and with peace in my heart. Tears were allowed, however.

We did release him, and more than ten years later, he and his growing family still live in LA. We miss him terribly but know that He is in the center of God's will, and that is the place of his greatest happiness and ours. "Thanks be to God for this indescribable gift" (2 Corinthians 9:15).

~~~~~~

Our children still navigate their own paths. As we watch them, we continue to trust God and remain grateful. Praying for them was always important, but I often reminded myself that the children belong to God. He gave us the privilege to raise them. We had the responsibility to be careful and prayerful. Each child is a gift. They were not ours to keep but to love, teach, pray for, and allow God to guide.

Remembering that they belong to God not only helped me let them go, but it also kept me on my toes as a parent. I knew that Tim and I had a God-given responsibility to raise them for Him. God chose us to be their parents and entrusted them to us. The Lord taught us on this parenting path and gave us insight and wisdom—a parenting partnership made in heaven. As we learned to trust God, He gave us the stamina, wisdom, and joy to partner with Him. He filled our journey with fun. And we still have years of great memories to make ahead of us as our children now have their own families.

Chapter 7

~~~~

The Path of Change

One thing we can count on in life is that things will change. King Solomon said it best, and the Byrds sang it with their hit song "Turn! Turn! Turn!"

> To everything there is a season,
> A time for every purpose under heaven:
> A time to be born,
> And a time to die. (Ecclesiastes 3:1–2 NKJV)

"To *everything* there is a season." These two combined words—*every* and *thing*—promise that, like it or not, our lives will be filled with continual change. Some of us hate change, others embrace it, but all of us need to be ready for it. Like the seasons, change happens. What I don't always appreciate is that each change has a purpose. From the moment of our birth through our life to our death, changes affect our lives!

The path of change requires that we have open hearts and open minds and trust the ways God is leading. Of all the paths mentioned in the Bible, the path of change insists that we watch and pay attention to all that is happening around us. We need to be willing to adapt and adjust when God-given opportunities show up.

Some of the most obvious and purposeful changes happen as we watch our babies grow. We first get to know our babies by holding them close to us through the changes in infancy. My mother believes that God created babies to be held while they eat. Feeding an infant gives the mother and child a lifetime bonding experience. During that season, newborn babies grow and develop tremendously. Little smiles turn into big grins. They sit up and soon progress to crawling, walking, and then they are off and running. Each change prepares them for the next one.

When my children were young, I didn't want them to get older too quickly. I cherished each stage of motherhood. Holding a newborn was my favorite stage, inhaling her sweet baby breath as I cuddled her. Watching my five-month-old son sit in an infant seat and follow me with his eyes, giving me secretive smiles and coos, was another special time. Engaging with a one-and-a-half-year-old as she learned to piece words together. Holding the chubby hand of a three-year-old, watching a ten-year-old confidently run down the sports field—no matter the age, and no matter the stage, every single one was my favorite. The only thing I could have done without was the wave of emotions that rolled in with four daughters going through puberty.

This may sound ridiculous, but I was emotional as I dropped each child off for his or her first day of preschool. Tim had to do first grade alone because I didn't want to cry when they followed our school's tradition of patting the bulldog and then marching off to their first-grade class. No matter what grade my children entered, my eyes were watery behind the camera, snapping their "first day of school pictures." Each "first day" marked another year when my babies were growing up. Eventually, I grew to love and embrace the changes—it just took me some time to get used to the new stages.

I remember this well as I packed away our fourth daughter, Cally's, newborn clothes and blankets. I loved having and holding babies, and as I moved these little clothes out of the drawer, I held them and quietly cried. *This* was my favorite age. Remember? They *all* are my favorites.

When it comes to growing families, my mother gave me this advice: "Lisa, pray that the desire of God's heart for your family will be the desires of your heart. He knows the size for your perfect family. Ask Him." With tears in my eyes, holding on tightly to baby gowns and swaddle blankets, I knew that night that we probably weren't finished having children. God had one more baby that He was birthing in my heart. Like Mary in the gospel of Luke, I tucked it away and "pondered these things in my heart." (See Luke 2:19.)

Yes, after a year of pondering and diapers, I found myself pregnant with our fifth child. And when it was time for me to put away Abby's sweet newborn clothes, I sat at the same dresser filled with the same infant clothes and began to move them from the drawer to the plastic container.

Did I cry this time?

No, quite the opposite; I sang "Oh Happy Day" as I packed up Abby's things and gave them away. And just like that, I knew our family of seven was complete.

With so many changes in life, I often didn't know what to expect. But rather than freeze time, I needed to keep up with the pace of each change and celebrate it. Try as I may, I couldn't keep Abby as an infant forever. Having watched her four older siblings for the first months of life, she didn't want to be a newborn for very long. She wanted to keep up with the rest of the pack, and she did!

Life continued to change and I struggled to adjust to the changes in our family. Even after going through similar changes multiple times, they never got easier. When Tim escorted one of our beautiful daughters down the aisle, or Willis walked his bride out of the church, I wept with joy and with sadness—joy at the thrill of this change and sadness that the wonderful season of raising children was over. I loved the path of parenting and wondered, or worried, what the empty-nest season would hold for us.

Five children became ten people with ten grandchildren and counting! What happened? And it happened so fast!

Often, I don't embrace the changes; I simply pretend they haven't really happened. Sometimes I feel as if I am still a thirty-eight-year-old mother wrangling five children, but I sure don't look like one. I have changed and can't stop changing.

~~~~~~

As a girl, my earliest path to school changed several times between my house and the school. It started off bright as we ran down a hill, then became a little dark and ominous as we walked a dark wooded road that led to a steep and narrow uphill path. From the top of that path, we ran down another hill and finished our walk through a wide-open field to the school. Confident of the path, I would start running in freedom, walk in the darkness of the road, work hard to get up the narrow path to the top, then skip down the other side and through the field, only to find even this simple familiar path constantly changing. The topography changed and the weather would add to the changes. The time of day and the people on the journey with me all changed the path. I knew it so well, but it was rarely the same walk.

Water changes completely when the environment around it changes. When extremely cold, water becomes ice. When heated, it boils, and when heated more it becomes steam. Sometimes the changes of water threaten our established lives, and at other times, the changes are a relief.

95

A rainstorm can become an ice storm or even a blizzard. Or a rainstorm can be a long-awaited answer to prayer after a drought. The basic ingredients are the same, but as the surroundings and temperature change, so does the water. God created a world filled with a variety of changes.

As I raised my children, I experienced both the fear of change and the relief of change.

The best way for us to see and celebrate change is by watching the seasons. God has given us beautiful visuals as we witness spring evolving into summer, summer into fall, fall into winter, and the best is the change from winter to spring. Most of the world has seasonal changes. Some are dramatic, and in some locations, seasonal change is almost imperceptible.

And again, we look at the details in Ecclesiastes 3:1–8:

> To everything there is a season,
> A time for every purpose under heaven:
> A time to be born,
> And a time to die.

The scripture continues to describe change, not as physical seasons, but as the changes in the seasons of life. Please read this slowly and carefully. Because it is so familiar, I have a tendency to skim over it. Upon careful reflection, I could see that it is filled with deep and unique truth.

> A time to plant,
> And a time to pluck what is planted;
> A time to kill,
> And a time to heal;
> A time to break down,

And a time to build up;
A time to weep,
And a time to laugh;
A time to mourn,
And a time to dance;
A time to cast away stones,
And a time to gather stones;
A time to embrace,
And a time to refrain from embracing;
A time to gain,
And a time to lose;
A time to keep,
And a time to throw away;
A time to tear,
And a time to sew;
A time to keep silence,
And a time to speak;
A time to love,
And a time to hate;
A time of war,
And a time of peace.

This well-known passage has so many facets. Sometimes I read it for comfort as I watched the children change from preschool to high school and then on to their grown-up lives.

Sometimes it has encouraged me to grow as a changing family. In my life as a daughter, daughter-in-law, friend, or business associate, every relationship changes, and we must expect it and allow it.

For many generations, this passage has comforted parents who may have shed tears as they watched the seasons change in their children's lives, or even in their own lives.

Churchquake!

Of course children change! I expected and wanted those changes. But there was a change that took me completely by surprise, and that was the change in our church—maybe I would call it a churchquake?

We had attended our church for more than twenty years. It was the place where our children had been born, raised, baptized, confirmed, and hopefully would be married. We believed that God had called us there and we had no plans to leave, until one day everything changed.

It could be called the "perfect storm."

A combination of factors brought on the storm of destruction: a change in doctrine, the denominational leadership attacking our clergy, plus angry and frustrated members. Our large, well-attended church was reduced from about seven hundred on a Sunday morning to fewer than one hundred. A majority of the church staff departed, along with many of the church leaders, youth ministers, Sunday school teachers, nursery workers, and others.

I watched as dear friends whom I loved and respected hitched their wagons and hit the trail for greener pastures, and I desperately wanted to hop in one of their wagons and ride away. Frustrated, hurt, and confused, I cried out to God and asked Him to show us our next step on this path, which had radically changed in a few short months.

He didn't answer my prayer to leave in the way I expected and wanted (prayers like "Get me out of here!"), but He answered prayers that we should have prayed ("Thy will be done").

But God. Even in the tumult, division, and pain, God was still there! *But God*—two words that always get my attention!

God had another plan for us. My sweet husband reminded me that God had called us to join our church, and until God released us, we couldn't leave. He didn't believe we had been released, and to my disappointment, I agreed with him.

One summer Sunday morning, I obediently forced myself to go to our sad and mostly empty church. In the parking lot, I complained to the Lord, "I hate this! I don't want to be here. This isn't fun, and I am not happy here. I don't get anything out of the service, and this feels like a big waste of time. For all those reasons and more, I think it is time for us to leave this church. Please?" I dragged myself into the sanctuary, waiting for the service to begin and praying that it would end soon.

Our church has three distinctive parts in the format of the service: the reading of Scripture, the sermon, and holy Communion. If the sermon is slow, there are two other opportunities for God to speak to you. Usually I try to pay attention to what is happening in the church service. This day, however, I was not engaged in any part of the service.

As I sat there, I began to think about the women who had been a part of the Bible study I had taught for the past twenty years. Some had moved to other parts of the country and begun their own Bible studies; some had started Bible studies in their homes; others had changed churches and Bible studies. Some had just stopped coming, and some were still with me. The Bible study had changed, the church had changed, and we were being changed by all of this.

On this particular morning in our shattered church, my heart ached. Filled with discouragement, hurt, and confusion, I felt that all my years involved in the leadership of the Bible study and the church really hadn't mattered to God, the women, or me.

But God. God had a surprise for me. Right in the middle of one of my best pity parties, I saw the picture of a dandelion in full seed (to this day, this is the closest experience I have ever had to a vision). The seeds were all there, attached to the stem, and then a breeze started to gently blow the seeds. Some of the seeds moved as individual seeds; others moved together in a group of three to ten. The breeze blew most of them off the stem and far away.

Through this flower in seed, God spoke to my heart. I saw in my mind's eye that these seeds represented the work with the women of the Bible study. Some women moved away; some moved to another church; some were called by God to start their own ministries. Each change, each new venture, each new location—they were all good things! The Bible study ministry was God's work. *He* had made these little seeds, and He was planting them in other places. Instead of leaving me to feel that the women had left me or the church, God reassured me that He was planting them in other places. It was all part of His good plan, and He was still in control.

This whole vision didn't last very long, maybe ten seconds. I don't really know. But its impact brought me great understanding and freedom.

Even more amazing, I tuned back in to the church service and heard the Gospel reading for the day, Matthew 13:3–8:

> Listen! A farmer went out to plant some seeds. As he scattered them across his field, some seeds fell on a footpath, and the birds came and ate them. Other seeds fell on shallow soil with underlying rock. The seeds sprouted quickly because the soil was shallow. But the plants soon wilted under the hot sun, and since they didn't have deep roots, they died. Other seeds fell among thorns that grew up and choked out the tender plants. Still other seeds fell on fertile soil, and they produced a crop that was thirty, sixty, and even a hundred times as much as had been planted!

In a few seconds, God gave me so much peace about the church, our being there, and His past, present, and future plans for us there. The power of the reading of the parable of the sower and the seeds quickly changed my attitude and perspective.

Each seed fell on a different type of path. Each had a different result. Each seed was grown, scattered, and planted by the Master Gardener. The work was God's. My job was to listen to God's voice, pay attention, be obedient, and stay where God planted us.

In our broken church, without a minister, in the middle of a huge pity party, God spoke to me! He reminded me that He had not left our church and He had not left me. We were painfully aware that the path for our church had dramatically changed. God called us to keep moving forward and not to leave. That morning in church, His gentle Spirit gave me hope.

The picture of the dandelion filled me with peace and a sense of purpose. I continued to teach the smaller Bible study, and we became more committed to the church and its people. Like us, they were grieving too.

This story illustrates just how good our God is. On that Sunday, sitting in church, crippled by discouragement, not only did God speak to my heart with the vision of the dandelion, *but God*—He didn't stop there! He went on to confirm the vision with a perfect scripture. *That* is how good and perfect our God is.

As we lived on this path of change, we watched God move mountains. A traumatized church is a magnificent opportunity to see God at work. We trusted God, we stayed at our post, and we stood back and watched God do what He does—move in miraculous ways, rebuild that which has been broken, and transform old into new. *But God!*

~~~~~

While the vision gave me hope, weeks went by, and each Sunday the church felt bare and lifeless. I noticed that plenty of people in our neighborhood didn't go to any church. I wondered if there was a way to reach my neighbors. I didn't want to invite them to church directly, but maybe something else?

I had an idea that percolated in my head until one day I took a walk on the beach with my friend Jodie, who is always an inspiring confidante. We began to explore the options and uncovered a great plan. Being on the ocean's edge with a trusted and inspiring friend was so good for me.

The plan? Ten women could invite ten friends, neighbors, or coworkers to come for lunch at a country club to hear a culturally relevant Christian speaker share a meaningful story and message of hope. Two women, one idea, and "Changing Seasons" was born!

With the birth of Changing Seasons, we did not set out to model a Bible study; we wanted to be different. We wanted to create a warm and welcoming space where women, regardless of their backgrounds, would feel safe, comfortable, and loved. Instead of looking for your typical Bible teacher, we sought speakers whose messages transcended churches and Bible studies—speakers who would be good at garden club meetings, business gatherings, or community groups. At Changing Seasons, speakers could share stories from their lives and weave in a compelling Christian message of hope, giving women the opportunity to "taste and see that God is good!" (Psalm 34:8).

To help us define our goals, I had a picture in my mind. Bible study ladies are like fluffy sheep—beautiful, fluffy sheep. They know where all the Christian food is—Bible studies, prayer groups, women's gatherings, conferences—and they attend as many as possible because they love to be nourished by solid Christian food.

Let's call these beautiful, fluffy sheep the "fat sheep." Each "fat sheep" has "skinny" friends who might not go to their local church or wouldn't know where or how to find a Bible study. Their book clubs, hospital service groups, garden clubs, and tennis groups suit them just fine.

But what if some of these "skinny sheep" were looking for more meat and substance in their lives and just didn't know where to find it? What if they wanted hope, joy, and a reminder that God was always with them?

This was the inspiration for Changing Seasons. The name is not about aging or life's changes, but about the variety of seasons each woman encounters throughout her life. As seasons change throughout the year, so do life's circumstances. Some seasons are quiet, dormant, and maybe lonely. Other seasons are productive and action-packed.

Seasons change. Nothing lasts forever. Every good season will probably evolve into a more challenging season. The best news is that every hard season will eventually change too.

We wanted to bring in speakers who could discuss different seasons of life and give insights about how to navigate them. Our first speaker was a very popular news broadcaster; others included a Wimbledon tennis champion, reality TV stars, entrepreneurs, and mothers. Eleven years later and we're still going, fortifying women with stories of hope and joy.

For each event the goals are the same: first, the women attending are nourished and encouraged in their faith, and second, we don't lose money. The country club holds around two hundred women, and we have kept each event that size—big enough to be fun and small enough to be personal. From the first event, the goal of ten women with ten friends quickly grew to become eighteen to twenty-two women with their ten or more friends. We have stayed near capacity for every event.

God has led us on a wonderful journey with Changing Seasons. We haven't lost money, and lives have been touched and transformed by the work of the Lord. We have met some incredible and inspiring women. My journey with Changing Seasons has been an amazing, surprising path, birthed from an unexpected and difficult change. Yet another beautiful thing about our God—we can't discount God's ability to move in and through any type of change, even the ones we don't want. Even through difficult, fractured seasons, our God is "able to do exceedingly abundantly above all that we ask or think" (Ephesians 3:20 NKJV).

~~~~~~

Not only was a new ministry born out of this time of upheaval, but in case you're wondering, our church survived its "earthquake," or as I liked to call it, "churchquake."

Looking back on our church split, though initially an unwelcomed, painful transition, I don't know that I would change it. The shattered church family stood together with the Lord and witnessed several great miracles. Little by little we changed in the church. We prayed, cried, and dreamed together. We had to depend on God to lead us through this change. People who had previously irritated us became our treasured friends. We learned to appreciate each other as we navigated together the challenges of change.

God took our little church and breathed new life into its dry, tired bones. He brought a new team into the church with a God-given vision to move in our church, and it began to grow.

Eleven years ago, I sat in the pew feeling hopeless, wondering if our church could ever be rebuilt. *But God.* He's never finished. Only God can take our messes and turn them into miracles. And if that wasn't enough, He helped me channel some of my frustrations into a fruitful endeavor through Changing Seasons—a ministry that continues to encourage women.

Another great blessing of the churchquake was what our children learned by watching us. They saw God's faithfulness to our family and the church. They heard our questions, "Do we stay? Should we leave?" Now that they are having their own church experiences, they know it is important to ask God the same questions: "Is this the church you are calling us to attend?" Or if they are struggling with church life, they know that before they flee, they need to ask, "Lord, is it time for me to leave?" Wait, pay attention, and watch to see God's answer.

Jesus is the same yesterday, today, and forever. He never changes, but we will change and grow. Change is inevitable in every part of life. The best way for me to grow with the changes is to pay attention to the Lord's leading. Isaiah promised us: "Your own ears will hear him. Right behind you a voice will say, 'This is the way you should go,' whether to the right or to the left" (Isaiah 30:21). Is His quiet voice speaking to me? What is my next step on the path?

"To everything there is a season, a time for every purpose under heaven." According to the wisdom of King Solomon, everything has a season and a purpose. God is efficient and doesn't waste His works. All things can work for good.

One of the most treasured verses in the New Testament, Romans 8:28, states, "And we know that God causes everything to work together for the good of those who love God and are called according to his purpose for them." God is the God of the resurrection and new life! What He does so well is bring His abundant life to our lives. In the changes of life, I try to look for opportunities, growth, and maybe even a little fruit.

Now that I am a grandmother, I am thankful that I no longer have five children who are eight years old and under. I loved that season of raising children, but this season is much better. Changes happen; seasons change. Look for the changes in the seasons of life. There is no reason to be intimidated by them, and I am learning to choose to trust God with change. I see that He is faithful to lead me on the best path for my life, and I have grown to celebrate the changes (most of the time!).

Ready or not, here they come!

Chapter 8

~~~~~

The Path of Joy

In Your presence is fullness of joy;
In Your right hand there are pleasures forever.

—*Psalm 16:11* NASB

As we've already seen, the first promise of Psalm 16:11 is that God has a path and He will show it to us. The next two promises are equally clear:

- In His presence there is fullness of joy.
- In His right hand there are pleasures forever.

But what does it mean to be "in His presence," and how do we know when we are there?

Tough questions, but important ones to ask to help us understand the promises of Psalm 16.

The first answer is simple: we are *always* in His presence. The Bible is very clear; God will never leave us nor forsake us (Hebrews 13:5). Scripture also assures us that nothing will separate us from the love of God (Romans 8:35–39). No, not ever!

Answering the above question is easy, but the problem is this: even though I "know" I'm always in God's presence, I don't always feel the presence of God, nor do I always feel the fullness of joy Psalm 16 describes. But in walking with God for many years, here's what I've discovered: just because I don't feel something doesn't mean it isn't there. Feelings can deceive us. They are not always the truth.

Feelings are fickle; they are influenced by moods, circumstances, the weather. Even a television show or a song on the radio can swing your pendulum of emotion. Allowing my feelings to have too much influence is not only immature, but it's dangerous. Rather than allow our feelings to be dictated by our surroundings, we should view them as fruit on a tree—fruit that will mature and grow, simply by being attached to the tree. God is the source of our growth and life. With God as our stability, our joy should continue to mature and grow, no matter the surroundings. Giving our emotions too much influence in our lives can lead us to believe things that aren't true.

Early in our marriage, I learned how easy it was for me to allow my fickle feelings to determine how I reacted to Tim. One fall afternoon, we had an argument, and in my mature way, I decided to "punish" Tim by giving him the silent treatment. All Sunday afternoon, I didn't say a word to him. I huffed and puffed, quiet on the outside but boiling on the inside. My big mistake was that this happened during football season, and he was so engrossed in his beloved Redskins that he wasn't aware of my silence. After several hours, my feelings were hurt and I didn't think Tim cared, but the reality was that he didn't even know.

Tim will tell you that he had a very peaceful afternoon, and I will tell you that the longer I gave him the silent treatment, the madder I got. I slammed a few pots as I washed the dishes, hoping to get his attention, but no response.

I felt that Tim had hurt my feelings; Tim felt happy and relaxed as he watched a great football game.

Not only was my silent treatment ineffective, but I wasted an entire Sunday afternoon huffing and puffing about. We've grown through the years in how we communicate and resolve conflict, but I'll tell you one thing: Tim will never get the silent treatment again.

Rather than manufacturing the right feelings, if we want to truly be filled with joy in God's presence, we need to know that this joy is a gift from God, plain and simple. There's nothing we can do or strive toward; we don't *achieve* fullness of joy, but as a gift, we *receive* it. If I could work to receive the fullness of joy, I would work hard because I want it. If we try to make attaining "fullness of joy" about our hard work, it becomes all about effort and accomplishment and is no longer God's gift.

Truthfully, it might be easier for me to work for joy than to just receive it, regardless of my circumstances. But thankfully, no matter what our circumstances may be, when we pay attention and open our eyes to see God's presence all around us, at every moment, the gift of His fullness of joy is not far behind.

Choose Joy

Joy doesn't necessarily mean happiness. Happiness is more of a fleeting emotion; it comes and goes, depending on the world or life events that surround me. My happiness is easily influenced by what is happening around me. Like all feelings, happiness is fickle.

On the other hand, joy is a resolute emotion. It is an attitude and inspires confidence and contentment. It depends on God and nothing else. God is the source of true joy. Joy comes when we are confident that He is the God of our lives, He has a plan, and if we stick close to Him, we will find it. This assurance of God's way results in joy, strength, and courage.

Throughout the Bible, many writers teach us about joy. Nehemiah 8:10 states, "Do not grieve, for the *joy* of the Lord is your strength" (NIV). Because of the classic Sunday school song, "The Joy of the Lord Is Your Strength," our children learned to love this song from Nehemiah. It has always surprised me that this happy verse is preceded by the words "Do not grieve."

Nehemiah wrote the words *grieve* and *joy* in the same sentence. They seem to be opposites, but here Nehemiah links them together. Nehemiah is well-known for his leadership in the rebuilding of the walls of the city of Jerusalem. In those circumstances—returning to a crumbling, defenseless city after years of exile—there were reasons for the people to grieve. Yet they were encouraged to be strengthened by joy, not weakened by grief and discouragement. Their joy was in the presence and power of God, not their frightening circumstances. They chose to receive joy. Their joy was in knowing that God was with them.

The New Testament repeats this teaching:

Always be full of joy in the Lord. I say it again—rejoice! Let everyone see that you are considerate in all you do. Remember, the Lord is coming soon. Don't worry about anything; instead, pray about everything. Tell God what you need, and thank him for all he has done. Then you will experience God's peace, which exceeds anything we can understand. His peace will guard your hearts and minds as you live in Christ Jesus. And now, dear brothers and sisters, one final thing. Fix your thoughts on what is true, and honorable, and right, and pure, and lovely, and admirable. Think about things that are excellent and worthy of praise. Keep putting into practice all you learned and received from me—everything you heard from me and saw me doing. Then the God of peace will be with you. (Philippians 4:4–9)

The strength is from God; joy is ours as we know and follow Him. This gift of joy and strength gives us confidence in God's great love for His treasured children. The result is described in Psalm 19:8, which tells us that God's instructions make our hearts rejoice and our eyes shine.

Raising my young family, I needed both the joy and, especially, the strength. As a teacher for the weekly Bible study, I learned that the best and often only time that I was able to prepare the lesson was first thing in the morning, before the children were awake. The words of Psalm 90:14 helped motivate me to get up and begin my reading: "Satisfy us in the morning with your unfailing love, so we may sing for joy at the end of our lives." Morning by morning, I would meet with God. Most of the time, I didn't feel as if I had been given any divine inspiration or deep insight. The mornings with God were like eating breakfast. It was something I knew I needed to do, and it was important to me. Every day I would try to spend this time with God, reading a short passage from the Bible and saying a little prayer. The surprise was that I didn't feel anything or have many "aha" moments. But slowly and surely, as I invested my time, I sensed that this investment with God was making a difference in my life. Nothing specific, but I was changing.

You already know my favorite prayers: "Lord, show me . . . teach me . . . lead me . . . guide me . . ." When I begin my day seeking the Lord first, my eyes and heart are more open to His leading in my life. God's presence filters my thoughts and reactions. His words and teaching become a delight to my soul, and walking in His commands is life-giving.

When I don't start with the Lord, my thoughts and reactions filter God, and I find myself resisting His promptings and leadings.

One particular morning I was especially rude, impatient, and angry. My sweet husband asked me, "Did you have your quiet time this morning?" The very idea that he would ask me was so irritating because I took great pride in the fact that he wasn't nearly as diligent with his faith as I was with mine.

"No!" I snapped.

He quietly replied, "I can tell."

Of course he was right, and it made my blood boil. But to my surprise, I understood that the investment of my time with the Lord made a difference not only to me but also to those around me. This was irritating and encouraging; Tim could see that I had lost my joy in the Lord and I could see that my investment of time in the morning mattered to me and the family.

On another day, I was trying to fast (or maybe diet). The children were increasingly frustrating to me. There was little joy in me that day. Because she was afraid to ask me in person, Laura, age eight, wrote me a note in her best handwriting: "Mommy, why are you so mean? Would you please eat?"

I ate and thanked her. The Holy Spirit was not controlling my life that day. I was. What a big difference in the fruit that I produced—I was impatient, cranky, and rude. I craved the fruit of the Holy Spirit and wanted it to grow.

When I miss the early time with the Lord, people, circumstances, and frustrations filter my day and my time with the Lord. The choice is mine: either filter the day with the presence of God or with the chaos of the daily news and my family.

Being anchored with God makes such a difference in my attitude and has enabled me to sing for joy all my days, even when I'm not happy. Sometimes we just have to make the decision to show up and let God do what He does.

~~~~~

"Make me walk along the path of your commands," Psalm 119:35 tells us, "for that is where my happiness is found." Because we know God is always with us, we must also be aware that His presence is fortified as we choose to follow Him day by day. This verse tells us that our joy is found as we walk the path of God's commands. Many people misunderstand the purpose of God's commands. They are not to hold us back; they are to set us free. God designed His commands to benefit, bless, and fill our lives, not to withhold His blessings.

Have you ever driven a winding mountain pass? Do you remember the signs posted on the road? Dangerous Curve, Slow, Safe Speed, 25 MPH, No Passing, and others. These are signs to save your life and help you successfully navigate a difficult road.

The Ten Commandments and the Great Commandment are like these road signs. They warn, guide, and protect us. Instead of resenting them and feeling that God is depriving us, we should be grateful for their wisdom and their truth. The "path of God's commands" not only brings us joy, but also security, safety, and peace.

Choosing Joy

"You crown the year with a bountiful harvest; even the hard pathways overflow with abundance," says Psalms 65:11. Some days, when I don't feel the joy, joy becomes my choice. When I make the decision to trust God, I am confident that, no matter what unfolds, eventually I *will* find joy in His presence. And as I've walked with God, I've had to learn to rest in His joy and trust Him, even when life's situations are imperfect and hard.

Joy is a word that I have always associated with my youngest daughter, Abigail (Abby). Her name means "the father's joy" or "the father rejoices." Like me, she has blonde hair, always standing out in a sea of redheaded siblings. She affectionately refers to the two of us as the "blondetourage." Like me, she loves skiing and adventure, and is always up for a good dance party. And like me, she was born missing two teeth—the ones in between her front teeth and her canines.

Following her graduation from college, the ideal time presented itself to take the steps to fix her teeth. Having done this with three other children, I knew there were a variety of options, from dentures to bridges or implants. The procedure is routine, simple, and expensive. My teeth were fixed when I was her age, as were her siblings', and now it was her turn.

We met with our family dentist to discuss options and dental specialists. We decided that two dental implants would be the best route for her. There were two possible dentists to do this work. One was an older, established, well-known dentist, and the other was younger, well educated, and had the latest and best equipment. Because our family dentist had worked closely with the younger dentist and he had full confidence in his friend, we chose him.

What should have been a simple process taking no longer than a year evolved into a six-year drama. Many days it felt as if it would never end. After extensive dental work, including braces, gum grafts, and implants, the simple problem became increasingly difficult because of serious mistakes made by the younger, fancier dentist.

In spring 2014, the dentist told Abby she was ready for the two veneers for implants. She finally heard the words she had longed to hear: "You are ready for the final step." In June, Abby was going to be a bridesmaid, and for the first time in her life, she would have a perfect smile.

With a big grin on her face, she returned to our family dentist for the final procedure. She sat in his chair and opened her mouth. In the words of our family dentist's wife, "He looked at her teeth and wanted to cry. He had to leave the room to compose himself. He couldn't believe what he saw."

Abby had been severely damaged by the specialist's work. In his attempt to do the simple procedure for the implants, his work destroyed the bone and gums that held six of her front teeth.

The words "You are ready for the final step" had brought joy and relief to Abby, but in fact, those words were wrong. The specialist had failed, and without even admitting the problem, he returned the patient whose mouth he had destroyed back to his friend, our family dentist. After two years of work and thousands of dollars, instead of success, Abby had a severely damaged mouth.

The harder journey began, a difficult path. After tears, anger, and frustration, we called on an older dentist, the one who had solved this missing-teeth problem with our first daughter.

Dr. Bachman was happy to see us again. He looked at Abby's mouth and quickly told us that her issues were so serious that no dentist in our city had the skills required to produce the result we wanted. He referred us to some of the best-trained dentists on the East Coast. After some research, we took our first trip to Atlanta to visit some preeminent cosmetic dentists, not knowing what to expect when we arrived. But being the optimists that we are, we hoped for an easy solution.

I had a consultation with one of the nurses, and she commented, "I can't believe what that dentist did to her." After reviewing the damages, this premier dental practice announced that even they were not able to give Abby the best results. They suggested we begin her treatment with world-renowned specialists in Florida and then return to Atlanta for her final procedures.

The Florida group specialized in complex reconstructive and implant cases. Doctors throughout the world consult and refer to Dr. Johnson. He lectures worldwide, writes for medical journals, teaches, and advises top dentists about their most difficult cases. So there we were, in beautiful Sarasota, in the care of a brilliant dentist.

Because the bone had been destroyed, Dr. Johnson began

immediately with a plan to stop the deterioration and begin the restoration. This required a bone graft—taking bone from Abby's hip and planting it in her mouth. (Doesn't this remind you of the angel touching Jacob's hip in Genesis 32:25?)

I latched on to an inspiring quote I'd read somewhere: "The pessimist sees the difficulty in every opportunity; the optimist sees opportunity in every difficulty."

Because we had no other option, we determined that this was an opportunity for God. I can't tell you how many times a dentist or a nurse told us that this was a "very special case." As her mother, I always knew Abby was special, but this was never the special I had in mind.

At the beginning of 2016, the word that the Lord put before me was, "Will you trust me?" I was trying to trust God, but disappointment and confusion blanketed me. Things were not turning out the way I wanted, expected, or prayed for. The journey was a walk through a long valley. Abby maintained her joy-filled hope.

In April 2016, Abby was admitted to a surgical hospital in Florida to undergo her bone implant. They cut the bone from her left hip and grafted it into the top of her mouth so they could replace the six teeth she had lost (two missing by genetics, four pulled to prepare for the bone graft).

After several days in Florida, we returned home. Because of the bone implant, Abby was on crutches, and yet she still had a smile. We prayed and waited for the fusion of the graft. At this point in our journey, we had done everything we knew to do. Cell phone numbers of some of the best dentists in the world were now in Abby's contact list. All we could do was pray and wait.

A few more trips back to Sarasota, and in August we learned that her graft had healed 75 percent; 25 percent had failed. Then the news came that of the healed 75 percent, only 50 percent was able to receive the needed implant screws.

I was so discouraged. "Lord, are You telling me that after four years and tens of thousands of dollars, we've only gained 50 percent success? God, You can do better than that. Please! We have done all we know to do. I know You can help her. Why aren't You?"

To me, it was one long, dark valley. I am a Bible teacher. For more than thirty years I have encouraged women to trust in the Lord, to pray without ceasing, and to thank God in everything. I have known and taught on the faithfulness of God. We are His children. He is our Father, who knows us better than anyone does and loves us more than anyone will ever love us. I have always felt that I was one of His favorite children, because why wouldn't I be? We are all His favorites!

In this season, however, I felt the door to heaven was closed to me. Yes, I continued to teach and proclaim (and believe) in the mightiness and great love of God for us, but for the first time I could remember, I felt as if He didn't hear or answer my prayers.

Abby went back to Atlanta for another bone graft. Instead of her hip, they used bone from a cadaver and bone protein. Another surgery, more time in the hotel. Discouragement and disappointment set in, but to my relief, Abby remained optimistic, happy, and confident. This was an answer to prayer.

But God—He is amazing. In September our Bible study started teaching the book of Psalms. There, I learned that David experienced discouragement and disappointment too. He also had felt that God had closed the door to his prayers. "Why am I so discouraged? Why am I depressed?" These were David's questions and mine.

Even in the pit of desperation, David praised the Lord and sang his prayers. David followed his questions with the declaration, "I will yet praise him" (Psalm 42:5, 11; 43:5). He chose to give God thanks and glory. He sang of the mercies and love of the Lord. As I read the psalms and taught about David, I knew the Lord had some things for me to learn.

When I wanted to say:

I hate this and I don't understand. I am so discouraged and disappointed. You promised that You would never leave me nor forsake me. You taught me that where two or more agree in prayer, it would be done for them. You are the Great Physician. You are the God who heals, You love Abby more than we do, and she is suffering. We are here because of an arrogant, incompetent, and deceptive dentist. WHERE ARE YOU?

I would quickly follow with words like:

Thank You, Lord, that You are with us.
Thank You that You know the beginning from the end; thank You that Abby is Your precious child and that You love her. Thank You that this is not a surprise to You. You are God Almighty! You have prepared our path, and we are on it. Your path has a destination, and we can trust You in every detail. Thank You for Your great love and Your perfect plan.

Once again, I had to learn the power of praise. This is one of the most important components of the Christian faith. When we give thanks in all things, our hearts and our minds will change. In praising God, my expectations turn to God, rather than to the people or circumstances that surround me. Psalm 100:4 is so specific about how we should approach God: "Enter his gates with thanksgiving; go into his courts with praise. Give thanks to him and praise his name."

I have learned that I should begin or enter my time with the Lord with thanksgiving and praise. I hate to admit that it is still an effort for me, because often I want to jump in with my stuff.

Reminding myself that God inhabits the praises of His people (Psalm 22:3), I chose to praise and thank God. It wasn't always easy. Doing this enabled me to trust God in everything. I was determined to try to trust Him with Abby.

By changing the tone of my prayer from frustration and complaining to gratitude, the disappointment and discouragement turned into a miraculous joy. This gift of joy, knowing that God was with me, became my strength and my song. When I decided to trust God, my prayers changed. I even started to make up a tune and sing my prayers and the psalms. Singing became its own miracle. God gave us the gift of song to worship Him, and worship unlocks our hearts and spirits. When I made myself sing, my heart became more peaceful. I am not a good singer, but I do know how to make a joyful noise to the Lord (Psalm 98:4 and 100:1).

In the weeks that followed Abby's second bone graft, I was refreshed by the power of praise and the gift of singing. I believe that part of this journey was to remind me of the presence, the power, and the gifts of God. I was determined to trust Him, and singing and giving thanks helped me. He has given us the way to know His love and faithfulness, even when life is difficult. God is there. Have you ever heard the song "Amazing Love"? "Amazing love, how can it be, that You, my King, would die for me?"[1] This was how I felt. And that joyful feeling in the midst of discouragement, in and of itself, was a miracle.

Little did I know that this story was only going to get better!

After months of surgeries and disappointments, we pressed on. We still heard words like, "This is extremely unusual in a woman so young."

I continued to hope and wait for words of healing.

One evening in November, Abby called and described pus-filled blisters that had just formed in her mouth. She was in Atlanta for her follow-up appointment, but before she saw the dentist, she discovered the blisters. We all knew there was nothing routine about these blisters. Abby also called her dentist and, to prepare him for what he would see in the morning, she sent him photos of the blisters.

With heavy hearts, Abby and her friend Caitlin left the following morning for the dreaded dental appointment. Before leaving Caitlin's apartment, Abby had checked and all the blisters were still there. In the long, quiet car ride to the dentist, Caitlin, the most optimistic friend I know, tried to cheer them both up. But not surprisingly, they arrived at the dentist's office worried and fearful.

When Abby was called back, she sat in the chair and opened her mouth. The dentist seemed confused as he said, "I can't believe it. I can't believe what I am seeing." He left Abby alone in the room and called for his colleagues. They all looked at the photos on his phone that Abby had sent the previous day and compared them with her mouth as they were looking at it now.

Three other dentists, and their assistants, all gathered and stared. Without saying anything, they handed her a mirror, and to Abby's shock and theirs, she saw that *all the blisters were gone.*

A *miracle*—all the blisters were gone! I am not sure who was the most surprised—Abby, her mother, or the dentist. There was no known reason why they disappeared. As Abby prepared to leave the office, our favorite dentist told Abby his opinion as to what had happened.

"Abby, you have just seen a miracle."

There was so much for us to learn through this. For me, I could hear the question from months ago, lingering in my thoughts, *Will You trust me?*

Trusting God was my choice. I felt that God had asked me if I could trust Him and if I would trust Him. Without knowing how this story would end, I began to trust by thanking Him and singing unto Him.

I sang to remind myself of the truths that I knew about God:

> Thank You, God, that You have everything under control.
> Thank You that nothing can separate us from Your love.
> Thank You that You love Abby more than we do,
> and You love her more than we are capable of loving her.
> You are the Great Physician, the Comforter, almighty God.
> I do trust You because I believe that You are good
> and able to be trusted with every detail of my life.

Again I learned that He is trustworthy.

I also learned more about joy, and about the promise that the joy of the Lord is truly our greatest strength. God gave me the gift of joy. This joy existed simply because of the certainty that God was with us. I was not happy about these circumstances, but His gift of joy fueled my courage and confidence to keep going, to keep thanking God, and to keep watching for the ways He was moving. I knew He hadn't left us. Even when I couldn't see Him, I knew He was still with us.

"When troubles of any kind come your way, consider it an opportunity for great joy," the apostle James wrote. "For you know that when your faith is tested, your endurance has a chance to grow. So let it grow, for when your endurance is fully developed, you will be perfect and complete, needing nothing" (James 1:2–4). Don't you love the reminder that our joy grows? Things that grow typically get stronger and bigger.

The gift of joy grows into our strength of joy. The Lord is always with us, but when we partner with Him and pay attention, the confidence of His presence empowers us with courage and joy. Knowing that the joy of the Lord is our strength helps us grow from just receiving the gift of joy to bearing the fruit of joy.

Psalm 92:14 says that the righteous "will still bear fruit in old age, they will stay fresh and green" (NIV). Not only is joy a gift from God; it is also a fruit of the Spirit (Galatians 5:22). The fruit of joy doesn't just appear in our lives; it grows. In the orchards and vineyards where fruit is grown, the trees are cultivated, fed, protected, watered, and cared for. Fruit grows, matures, and ripens.

When I was a young mother, I took a trip to Southern California. One day we drove by an orange orchard. According to the orange growers, an orange tree could live for more than a century and often produce fruit for more than fifty years. It is not unusual for one tree to produce three hundred oranges per year. Do the math—one tree, productive for more than fifty years, three hundred oranges a year—equals fifteen thousand oranges. The oranges have seeds, and if their seeds reproduce, it is impossible to know the bounty of one tree in an old orchard. How many oranges are produced throughout the life of an orchard? Possibly millions—there is no way to know for sure.

On that sunny day, I noticed a particularly gnarly and ugly tree, and it was full of beautiful fruit. My driver told me that these were especially old orange trees and their fruit was especially sweet. I took a snapshot in my brain of that tree, because I knew that it was a picture of what I wanted to be as I grew older—sweet and fruit filled.

Like the fruit of the world, the fruit of the Spirit blossoms and grows into fruit when we are connected to a branch or a vine. In the Christian faith, we are taught that we must be connected to Christ through the Holy Spirit. To help the children learn all the fruit of the Spirit, we made up a tune for this verse and the children loved to sing this family song: "But when the Holy Spirit controls your life, He will produce this kind of fruit in us: love, joy, peace, patience, kindness goodness, gentleness, faithfulness and self-control!" (based on Galatians 5:22).

(For those of you who want to learn this verse, please notice that the first three fruits have one syllable, the second three fruits have two syllables, and the third three fruits have three syllables! Isn't that clever?)

Joy comes to us when the Holy Spirit controls our lives. God is the source of our joy. Through the Holy Spirit, He creates, cultivates, and produces joy. There is no other source of true joy than the joy of the Lord, and that joy gives us strength to live each day. The fruit of joy grows when it is connected to the source of life and is given the time and space to mature and ripen. God plants the seeds and causes the fruit to grow. Fruit contains seeds, so fruit produces more fruit. Remember that as we grow the fruit of the Spirit, it is not about our striving and hard work; it's about staying connected to the source of life and growth.

~~~~~

Jesus came to "bestow on [those who grieve] a crown of beauty instead of ashes, the oil of joy instead of mourning, and a garment of praise instead of a spirit of despair" (Isaiah 61:3 NIV). The gift of joy is most apparent when we are unhappy about what is happening in our lives. Life is filled with heartache and trials. When you are in the midst of these, that's when you will discover the strength of joy. As we've said, joy is a gift to us from God. We cannot achieve joy; we must graciously receive it.

I have a special young friend named Mary Elizabeth. Without a doubt, she is one of the most beautiful girls I know inside and out. She married one of our children's favorite friends, and we knew that this perfect, beautiful couple was going to live "happily ever after." This couple seemed to have it all. They were beautiful, fun to be around, engaging, genuine, and they had a community who adored them and a marriage rooted in a strong faith.

As a mother to four girls, I quickly scooped Mary Elizabeth up and took her in as one of my own when she moved away from her family in Atlanta to Virginia Beach to be with her new husband. She was away from her mother, most of my girls were off at college or living away, and bringing Mary Elizabeth into my mother's nest was a delight.

When Mary Elizabeth and Meade announced they were pregnant with their first child, everyone was thrilled to watch this growing family blossom, especially when it was announced that they were having twin boys! What joy and what a gift. Mary Elizabeth devoted her life to carrying these boys, endured a long stretch on bed rest, and triumphantly made it to term, delivering two healthy, beautiful baby boys. Shortly after their delivery, however, their world was permanently rocked. She described it this way:

After a difficult pregnancy including hemorrhaging and five months of bed rest, we thought the worst was over as we delivered full-term and seemingly healthy identical twins in January of 2009. However, on their second day of life, both Warren and John began suffering from inexplicable and relentless seizures. Our world crashed around us as we were introduced to our children on January 21 only to have them ripped away from us on January 22 by incubators, wires, ventilators, and heavily sedating medication.

At that time, I received a phone call from Mary Elizabeth asking me to pray. Through her tears, I could hardly understand what she was saying, but I heard enough to know that I needed to go to the hospital as soon as possible.

The small, helpless boys seemed to be doing well when I first saw them, but things were about to change.

When we thought it could not get any worse, Warren died and went to heaven on February 8 at nineteen days old. Through the autopsy (which we had ordered to try to get answers to help John survive), we learned Warren actually died due to a medical error in which one of his oral medications was placed into his IV. This clotted in his lungs and shut off the oxygen to the rest of his body.

The crisis continued as John remained in the hospital . . . until he finally came home on April 17. John has done so much better than anyone imagined or predicted. Doctors told me he was going to die soon, never smile or develop at all, and need a G-tube to receive nourishment. He smiles all the time, is developing, and eats and drinks like a champ!

As I watched and prayed for this new mother grieving the loss of one son and struggling to fight for the life of another, for some strange reason, I kept thinking about the words in the Bible that describe a garment of praise for the spirit of heaviness (Isaiah 61:3).

Easter was coming up, and without giving it too much thought, I thought that Mary Elizabeth might need a garment of praise. So, I decided to take her to my home away from home: T. J. Maxx. Before we went in, we prayed that God would provide Mary Elizabeth the perfect garment of praise. We walked in, and before we'd even looked far, there it was! A beautiful, vibrant sundress by Tibi, which fit Mary Elizabeth perfectly. (Can I get an amen from all my fellow "Maxxinistas"?) I love how God cares about the big and small details of our lives—He knew just what Mary Elizabeth needed in that moment, and He made it happen! And isn't it just a little sweeter when it's on sale!

The picture of Mary Elizabeth and Meade that Easter Sunday will forever be seared in my brain, as she proudly put on her garment of praise, choosing joy in the midst of the most horrific battle of her little family's life. Mary Elizabeth made the decision to go to church and choose joy. She knew that Jesus didn't just die—He rose again; He conquered death on the cross. He suffered, died, rose again, and gave us all the promise that death does not have the final say—in Jesus, and because of Jesus, all things are made new (Revelation 21:5).

It seems to be a contradiction, a mystery when we are challenged to praise and thank God in the midst of a deep, dark valley. And yet, we are taught to give thanks in everything, to continually praise and thank God, even when our world is shattered. Why?

Does God need the reminder that we are grateful? No! We need the reminder that He has everything under control. He knows the beginning from the end; He will not withhold any good thing from His children. When we thank the Lord, our hearts are opened to His sweet presence.

Five days later, Mary Elizabeth and Meade brought their sweet baby boy John home from the hospital. A major victory in a long, hard fight. Thanks be to God! Ten years later, and three more adventurous, joy-filled boys added to the brood, Meade and Mary Elizabeth still struggle, but they remain connected to the Source, marked by the joy of the Lord. John is ten now and the family is filled with mighty warriors for the kingdom of God. Mary Elizabeth has never stopped fighting for her son—ensuring he receives the best schooling, therapy, treatments, medicines, therapy equipment, doctors—"Tiger mom" doesn't even come close to describing how relentless this mama is in fighting for her son. She even helped start a new location for a school for children with special needs to give more children like John access to an excellent education—all while mothering *four* boys! And it's God's joy that continues to strengthen her family along a hard and narrow path.

It's His joy that has given Mary Elizabeth strength to document and share her story, ministering to hearts along her journey. In 2012, Mary Elizabeth began a blog, appropriately named "He Makes All Things New," where she journals her life, struggles, faith, and insight. Her family's story has impacted thousands of lives as she has chosen to walk out the path of joy, even though her "happily ever after" looks different from what she originally envisioned.

> We miss Warren every single day but his life continues in heaven and on earth as we celebrate the gift God has given us through these precious twins. We long to be in heaven more than ever before, where all is redeemed and made new. However, we also realize God still has work for us to do on earth. As Paul said: "To live is Christ, to die is gain." Yes, when we die it will be a huge gain; while we are still alive, we trust God has a real and powerful purpose for our family. This has been the hardest and best year of our lives; in it all, we know God is faithful and He will never leave us nor forsake us.

~~~~~~

Joy comes when we get into God's presence. No matter what we may be facing, when we choose to enter into the presence of God, not only will we experience joy, but the Bible promises that we will be filled with joy. We can't forget that joy isn't something we achieve; it is something we receive from God. Joy is a gift from God that grows in our lives as we enter into His presence. It's His power and His presence in our lives that bring us joy.

True joy is found when we're anchored in God. When we choose to trust God and trust in His fullness of joy, we discover how the joy of the Lord strengthens us. True joy strengthens us, equipping us with courage and confidence.

No matter what season of life you may find yourself in, my prayer is that you will see the words of Psalm 30:5, "Weeping may go on all night, but joy comes in the morning."

As I type this, I'm praying Romans 15:13 over you: "May the God of hope fill you with all joy and peace as you trust in him, so that you may overflow with hope by the power of the Holy Spirit"! (NIV).

Chapter 9

~~

The Narrow Path

I will lead blind Israel down a new path,
guiding them along an unfamiliar way.
I will brighten the darkness before them
and smooth out the road ahead of them.
Yes, I will indeed do these things;
I will not forsake them.

—*Isaiah 42:16*

Most of us will walk on our own narrow paths. These paths are uniquely ours, designed by God for us. The narrow path sometimes is lonely, unknown, or even scary.

Discovering the narrow path takes experience. It doesn't have the neon sign flashing "Walk Here." It is found when we listen and follow the still, small voice that says something like, "Lisa, this is the way; walk in it" (Isaiah 30:21). In the same way we hold our cell phones in the air, searching for the optimal number of bars to strengthen our signal, we need to tune our spiritual ears to the voice of God, so when we hear, "This is the way," we are ready to go.

~~~~~

I want to look at several narrow paths in this chapter, but let's start with the most obvious narrow path that Christians find ourselves walking along: the narrow path to the kingdom of God. Jesus made it clear to us that we can only enter the kingdom of God through the narrow gate. He contrasts the narrow gate with the broad highway to hell.

> You can enter God's Kingdom only through the narrow gate. The highway to hell is broad, and its gate is wide for the many who choose that way. But the gateway to life is very narrow and the road is difficult, and only a few ever find it. (Matthew 7:13–14)

When we become Christians, our lives change. To live a life with Jesus at the center changes our focus. What used to be important to us, may not be as important. Before Christ was in my life some of the most important things to me were my friends, my social life, doing well in school, my family, having a job, and winning at tennis. After my introduction to Christ, Bible studies, church, and helping some ministries became more interesting to me.

Some of the changes were subtle and others were not so subtle, almost embarassing. I started thinking things like, *Lord, guide my thoughts today. Let me speak words that add to people's lives, not tear them down. Show me how to be a blessing to someone.* My thoughts, words, and deeds were changing because of the active presence of Christ in my life. Day by day, I hoped to please God by the way I lived. My perspectives changed as I tried to think more about God's ways for me. Forgiveness, peace, confidence, and even glimpses of eternity became part of my thoughts.

Even though I didn't fully understand the new me, I could feel myself changing. As described in 2 Corinthians 5:17, I was changing into a new creature in Christ—the old things were gone and new things came. At first it was a surprise to me; then it evolved into a "mountaintop" experience. To this day, my life has never been the same.

There is a saying that mountaintop experiences are beautiful and inspiring, but the fruit of life grows in the valley. (I like the mountaintops, but the fertile valleys might be more important to us.)

Several days after my tent-revival conversion, the emotion of the mountaintop subsided but my adventure on the narrow path continued. Instead of depending on my family or friends, I prayed and tried to faithfully follow the Lord. One afternoon, I was driving home on University Boulevard in Denver and passed a young man hitchhiking. I decided to turn around and pick him up so I could tell him my exciting news about havng Jesus in my life. Even though I knew that picking up hitchhikers was stupid and dangerous, I managed to believe that I was invincible from this danger because I was on a "mission from God."

I zipped around the block, prayed for the man, and looked for him. Mysteriously, he was gone. In my zealous disappointment, I thought I may have heard God say (or maybe it was it my own father?), "Don't you *ever* pick up a hitchhiker! Pray for hitchhikers as you drive by, but never stop to put them in your car!" I was trying to be full of faith and adventure. Wisdom and obedience were lacking that day. I learned how important it is for me to follow God and not try to manufacture a spiritual experience.

I learned the difference between my faith in God, not faith in my faith; obedience to God, not obedience to a notion. God was the leader on the narrow path, and I was learning to follow Him exclusively. As I leaned into my new life, the expression that described me is that I was so heavenly minded that I became no earthly good. My new enthusiasim changed me. My path became narrow, partly because I was a new creature in Christ and partly because I was too enthusiastic about sharing my faith with anyone, especially the ones I loved the most. Not all of them appreciated the new me.

As you might imagine, there were parts of my Christian life that were lonely. Some of my friends changed; my free time was invested in church or in Christian activities. Over the years, I have wondered why I had such a dramatic response to salvation. I believe that God used my public salvation experience so I would always remember His power. I never wondered if God had really come to me or if I had really accepted Christ, so I never looked back to return to my pre-Christ days. This was my first narrow path, and I knew God was with me, helping me adjust to this part of the path.

My new life as a Christian had its own challenges. As a new Christian, I was called to be set apart, to live a life that might look different from those around me. At times I was confused, vulnerable, and insecure. I knew in my heart that I was saved by grace, by a loving God, but hard questions still came up, especially when the darkness crept in and God felt distant. "God, where are You? I know You love me, but why are You allowing *this* to happen?" My questions never led me to doubt the loving presence of God, but I often doubted myself.

Choosing the narrow path of walking with Jesus may have been lonely at times, hard, or confusing, but it anchored me in the confidence that God was the center of my life. I was willing to change whatever I needed to live my life with Jesus at the center. I could never dream of going back to my old life. The challenges were real, but on this narrow path there was a strong sense of purpose that motivated me.

The narrow path asks us to trust God and His work in our lives. This way of living demands that we leave some of our old things behind: insecurities, people pleasing, worry, gossip, and more. These weigh us down on the journey. To my surprise, I discovered that I was more comfortable with my worries than I was trusting God. Sometimes, insecurities and worries were very familiar. Even though I am still certain that God wants His best for me, I am better able to receive His best when I choose to trust God, thank Him, and move forward, leaving the familiar insecurities and worries behind. This is a lifetime process, not a onetime event.

From my first days as a Christian, I have loved the description of Christians in 1 Peter 2:9: "But ye are a chosen generation, a royal priesthood, an holy nation, a peculiar people; that ye should shew forth the praises of him who hath called you out of darkness into his marvellous light" (KJV).

I longed to be chosen, royal, and holy. But so often I felt peculiar, and when I look back at some of my fellow believers, they were peculiar too. What a great word. I think it sounds like what it means: *peculiar*.

We first see the word *peculiar* in Deuteronomy 14:2: "For thou art an holy people unto the LORD thy God, and the LORD hath chosen thee to be a peculiar people unto himself, above all the nations that are upon the earth" (KJV).

The New Living Translation updated it: "You have been set apart as holy to the LORD your God, and he has chosen you from all the nations of the earth to be his own special treasure."

"He has chosen you . . . to be his own special treasure." What an image of love and assurance. I don't mind being called peculiar when it means I am God's special treasure.

This path may be narrow and a little peculiar, but make no mistake: this is the most life-giving decision we will ever make! Jesus came to give us abundant life—this doesn't always mean our lives will be easy, but walking with Jesus as His "special treasure" guarantees it will be abundant and full.

One of the challenges of the narrow path is staying the course. Sometimes, we long for change. Rather than sense God calling us out of a situation, raising us up to something new, we hear the message: "Stay the course."

In moments when we grow restless and discontented, the charge to "stay the course" can feel lonely and isolating, restricting and yet liberating.

I already shared in chapter 7 about our church split. In the heat of the moment, I didn't want to walk away from our church—I wanted to run. Yet my husband, who is much more even-keeled than I, continued to say, "Lisa, until God calls us out, we have to stay."

As hard as it was to honor Tim's decision, I knew he was right. This was our church, our family, our home for more than twenty-five years. We couldn't just jump ship when things fell apart; God had called us to stay, and we needed to hunker down and weather the storm with our church family.

One of the many blessings that grew out of that time was the way God's lesson for us cascaded down to our children. Our daughter Elizabeth wrote on her blog about how our decision impacted her life. It means so much to me to see how our actions indirectly impacted and taught her. Sometimes, when we're walking through a situation, we forget that our children see everything. This is one instance I'm glad she was paying attention. Here are Elizabeth's words:

Several years ago, my home church went through a very painful transition (as many churches, sadly, often do). I lived in Washington DC at the time so was more removed from the situation, but to see my beloved church, a church I had called home since I was two weeks old, walk through such tumult was incredibly painful.

When I returned home, rather than seeing many of the smiling faces I had become so accustomed to and comfortable with and revel in the life and joy that once poured through the doors, I saw empty pews, a struggling worship band, and an interim pastor. Make no mistake, there was still much life there, but you had to hunt for it.

Often, I would ask my parents, "Come on, guys, what are you doing? I think it's time to move on. There are so many great churches in the area, why are you STILL here?"

Their answer was always the same, "It's tempting to run to something else, but until God gives us something to run to and calls us away, we're not running away just because it's hard."

Their words will never leave me. Though it's often tempting, we need to be careful not to run from something, but wait until God gives us something to run to.

In my parents' case, that day never came. Rather, we watched in disbelief over God's goodness to bring our church an incredible new pastor with a fresh vision and passion for the church, raise up new leaders within the church community, and bring new families into the church.

It's hard for me to put into words just how clearly I've seen God's goodness carry our church through such a hard time, but often, it brings me to tears, because I just can't believe it. It's not just the fact that God brought one new pastor to us and all our problems went away; if I've learned anything through the highs and lows of one church's life through the years, it's that you can't put all your hopes in one man, because you'll inevitably be disappointed. It's the fact that it was easy to feel abandoned and hopeless, but even in the hardest, most lifeless times, God did not leave us.

Walking through this season with my family, I'm beyond grateful for the example my parents set for each of their five children. Rather than listening to the pleas from their children and many friends, they did not run away and they didn't jump ship.

They listened to the Lord, prayed for His insight, and waited patiently to see what God would do. And God DID!

In life, there are lots of times we want to flee when things get hard, painful, or take an abrupt turn. But we need to make sure we're tapped so tightly into God, that we're not just running away, but we're listening and waiting for Him to bring us something that we can run to. Sometimes He will, and other times, He calls us to stay the course, weather the storm, and watch and wait to see what He will do.

Running from something might be the expected and seemingly easier choice; but this time it was choosing to stay put that was the difficult, narrow path. In life, there are times when we need to run, but if we start running without a clear directive from God as to where we are headed, our efforts could be futile, might be a waste of time, or even could be destructive. At the end of the day we're tired from running, and we haven't even reached the right destination.

Staying put isn't always easy, but when we choose to follow the narrow path and stay planted, we may encounter God in new ways. Even when the situation feels old and stale, when we obediently stay and refuse to run, our eyes will open to new things. To our surprise, from our painful churchquake, we saw God move in mighty ways throughout our church and our lives. This is one of the times that I knew money couldn't buy the rich blessings we received from God by staying on the narrow path.

The Narrow Calling

There is one body, but it has many parts. But all its many parts make up one body. It is the same with Christ. We were all baptized by one Holy Spirit. And so we are formed into one body. It didn't matter whether we were Jews or Gentiles, slaves or free people. We were all given the same Spirit to drink. So the body is not made up of just one part. It has many parts. (1 Corinthians 12:12–14 NIRV)

I love how beautifully this passage depicts the body of Christ. All of us are baptized by one Holy Spirit, together we make up one body, but the body of Christ isn't made up of just one part; there are many. And no matter what role or assignment you've been given, often, walking out your calling can feel narrow.

As a mother to five children, I see this play out in different ways with each of the callings of their lives. All five of them grew in the same womb and were raised by the same mother and father, yet each one of them was uniquely formed and designed by God for specific things. Yes, there are many similarities between the five siblings (four have red hair), but there are also unique giftings and talents that God has specifically for each one. And God continues to lead each child on a narrow path that is uniquely theirs.

One mother, one father, five children—each gifted and called by their Creator to walk along the unique and narrow path He carves out for them. Budding entrepreneurs, struggling parents, involved in their schools, communities, and churches, each family is finding their own path.

One body, many parts. Ephesians 2:10 explains to us that we are God's "workmanship, created in Christ Jesus for good works, which God prepared beforehand that we should walk in them" (NKJV). Each one of us is uniquely created by God and for God. The narrow path of our calling may feel lonely or isolating, but we mustn't be discouraged about God's call. We are His workmanship! No matter what narrow path we find ourselves on, we can walk in confidence that the One who created us knows exactly where we need to be, and ultimately, He promises to fulfill the purposes He has for us (Psalm 138:8).

Travel Light

"Purify yourselves," we read in Joshua 3:5, "for tomorrow the LORD will do great wonders among you." As we discover our uniquely chosen paths, we may find there's some baggage that can't come with us. One requirement of the narrow path is that we shed the things in our lives that hinder our progress. This is often where the gentle voice of conviction comes into play. What may the Lord be quietly whispering to your heart to put down and let go?

All my life, I've worked to be skinny—diets, exercise, eating healthy, you name it! Traveling on the narrow path requires us to be spiritually fit—nimble and ready to live out the calling God has designed for us. To do that, we must examine the things that physically weigh us down, shed our excess weight, and prepare to travel light. That extra baggage weighing us down? It has to go!

This shedding looks different for everyone: it may be laying down the dreams and expectations you had for your life and surrendering them to God. For me, the shedding comes when God calls me to lay down certain sins and sanctify myself. Insecurities, people pleasing, anxiety, fear, gossiping, excesses—they have to go.

Like any diet or training regimen, traveling light requires discipline and obedience. But as we've already discussed, God asks us to put down and surrender those things to Him not to hurt us but to lighten us and make us nimble on the narrow path.

In every single thing, God is for us. Anything and everything that He asks us to leave behind is to help and free us. When God leads us to our narrow path, He wants us to be the best we can be;

He wants what is best for us and desires to give us His best. This is another place where we are challenged to trust Him and keep walking in obedience, and as we do so, we will discover new dimensions of His grace and His freedom.

Gather Your People

The best advice I can offer you on the narrow path is this: make sure that you are not walking alone. Get plugged in to a church and surround yourself with people who are running on the narrow path with you. Then, when the isolation, difficulty, or doubt creeps in, you have others in your life who can pull you up, speak truth, and pray for you.

What a relief and a gift it is that God did not intend for us to walk the narrow path alone—He gives us each other! Ecclesiastes 4:9–12 highlights the blessing and benefit of two in a relationship: "Two are better than one, because they have a good return for their labor: If either of them falls down, one can help the other up. . . . A cord of three strands is not [easily] broken" (NIV).

Jesus taught us the importance of being together when He said, "Where two or three gather in my name, there am I with them" (Matthew 18:20 NIV). What a wonderful promise. He is with us when we gather together in His name.

But even better than that? Jesus gives us Himself! When we become Christians, Jesus doesn't walk away, leaving us to fend for ourselves. He walks alongside us every step of the way, assuring us that He is with us until the end of the age.

But wait—there's more! So good and rich is our God, that He keeps going by giving us access to the Holy Spirit here on earth. In John 14, Jesus promised the gift of the Holy Spirit: "But the Advocate, the Holy Spirit, whom the Father will send in my name, will teach you all things and will remind you of everything I have said to you" (v. 25 NIV).

Accessing the Holy Spirit is a game changer. When the Holy Spirit takes over, nothing is off-limits. Through the Holy Spirit, we gain insight, revelations, visions, even new prayers to communicate and intercede with God. The Holy Spirit opens up our eyes and "guides us in all truth" (John 16:13).

To me, there is no passage in Scripture that encourages us on the narrow path as well as Hebrews 12:1:

> Therefore, since we are surrounded by such a huge crowd of witnesses to the life of faith, let us strip off every weight that slows us down, especially the sin that so easily trips us up. And let us run with endurance the race God has set before us. We do this by keeping our eyes on Jesus, the champion who initiates and perfects our faith.

Gather your people. Throw off your sin. Run the race God has set before you on your narrow path. Keep your eyes on Jesus—the One who both initiated your faith and perfects it.

Chapter 10

～～～

Potholes on the Path

You are my God. Show me
what you want me to do,
and let your gentle Spirit
lead me in the right path.

—*Psalm 143:10* (CEV)

Two words that often cause many of us to stumble on our path
are *condemnation* and *judgment*. Condemnation is represented by
the harsh, demeaning, and hurtful words we often hear in our heads.
Judgment manifests itself as thoughts that create the sense that we
or others will never be good enough. These destructive "potholes"
hinder and delay our progress. They attack our confidence and
they attack us. In our hurt, however, we fail to recognize that these
words are often lies from our enemy, Satan. Because God is our
defender, we don't have to allow them into our hearts, minds, and
lives. Our defense from these attacks is fought with God's truth,
which is most often the power and promises from the Bible.

Thankfully, each lie can be countered by the Holy Spirit's words
of truth and life. When accusations or feelings of condemnation fill

our minds, we don't have to let them settle in. God equips us with the resources to choose to reject them and instead listen to the life-giving truth of the Holy Spirit's conviction. When we are faced with destructive judgment, we must remind ourselves that these are lies designed to hurt us. We must learn about the gift of discernment. It will help us recognize the hurt and defend ourselves. Discernment is a spiritual gift from God listed in 1 Corinthians 12:10. Both conviction and discernment are gifts from God, designed not only to protect and strengthen us but also to empower us. Condemnation and judgment are lies capable of stealing the joy and strength God has given us. But we can fight against their potential destruction.

There's a fine line that separates *condemnation* and *judgment* from *conviction* and *discernment*. My goal in this chapter is to explore all four words, so we can avoid all potholes and confidently walk along the path filled with God's discernment and conviction. Hosea 14:9 states:

> Let those who are wise understand these things.
> Let those with discernment listen carefully.
> The paths of the LORD are true and right,
> and righteous people live by walking in them.
> But in those paths sinners stumble and fall.

The results of discernment and conviction are the work of God; they are to bring us truth and enrich our lives. Falling into judgment and condemnation is not from God. They derail our journey on the path of life and lead us to destruction. As we wrestle with understanding the difference between condemnation and judgment, we find God-given tools in the promises of His Word that protect our hearts and minds.

Let's begin with conviction. In all my years of teaching women, one lesson has resonated more than any other: the difference between the gentle and powerful conviction of the Holy Spirit and the destructive, angry words or thoughts that are really condemnation from Satan. Psalm 143:10 (CEV) describes the Holy Spirit's conviction perfectly: "You are my God. Show me what you want me to do, and let your gentle Spirit lead me in the right path."

The conviction of the Holy Spirit comes in gentle words. In my experience, the Holy Spirit speaks just a few words at a time. His words are both challenging and comforting and always constructive. The words of the Holy Spirit always enrich my life in a way that equips and fortifies me, providing guidance and directions to keep on the right path.

The Holy Spirit usually speaks to my heart, not audibly, but in a "still small voice," as the Bible describes it (1 Kings 19:12 KJV). These words can be an idea, a thought, or even a picture. Often it's so simple and quiet that even a child can recognize it. Recently one of my daughters was talking with her children about how to hear God. My five-year-old grandson was frustrated that he couldn't hear God's voice audibly. As they talked, my three-year-old granddaughter shouted, "Mommy! God told me something the other day! He told me that I'm going to be a mommy." No grandstanding, no shouting, just a small whisper from the Holy Spirit, *You're going to be a mommy.*

My daughter was shocked but confident that Virginia had heard the Holy Spirit's voice. This little girl lives and breathes baby dolls. Even at the age of three, Virginia is practicing and preparing for the dream of motherhood that the Holy Spirit whispered to her little heart.

Often, the Holy Spirit speaks to me in pictures that are so insightful I know they must be from God—I'm not that creative! One unusual picture came when I was praying with the CBN counseling center. I was one of about twenty-five people available to pray with viewers who called in for prayer. Some calls were from people who wanted to meet Christ; others were requests for prayer for family, financial, or marriage problems. For the first few days, I went home wearing the burdens of those who had called for prayer. The calls to accept Jesus were such great news, but many other calls made me so sad. The people had serious situations and wanted God's help in their crises. Having the prayer line was important and I enjoyed praying for the viewers, but often when I went home, I worried and continued to pray for them. Also, my inquiring mind wanted to know what happened after we prayed. How did God answer their prayers?

As I fretted over strangers, I saw a picture in my mind of a duck in the water. Not a sitting duck, but a swimming duck. The thought came to me, *Be like a duck when you pray with people. Don't absorb the problems. Bring them to Me, and I will care for them.* I thought about the difference between a sloppy sponge, which absorbs everything and doesn't clean well, and a duck, which swims freely and isn't weighed down by the saturation of water.

Instantly, I knew that I should simply pray for these callers, confidently asking the Lord to minister His truth and comfort. God loves them. He has the solutions for everyone, and He loves for us to ask Him. Absorbing their problems made me like a wet, sloppy sponge—messy, ineffective, and incapable of doing the job. I didn't want to be like the sponge, nor did God want me to be. I was to be like the duck—aware, involved, prayerful, concerned, but not weighed down.

God absorbs our problems for us. He carries our insecurities and reminds us that He is more than enough for us. "The Lord will perfect that which concerns me," David wrote with confidence. "Your mercy, O Lord, endures forever. Do not forsake the works of Your hands" (Psalm 138:8 NKJV). Our troubles don't weigh God down or make Him sloppy. In His love and concern,

He absorbs them. I have to be careful not to try to do the work of God. His plan and provision are perfect for all that we need.

A duck and a sloppy, wet sponge? I knew this was a picture from the Holy Spirit—there's no way I could come up with that insight on my own. I have found that His voice is constructive and leads me to understand some surprising things. The Holy Spirit speaks words of truth and life. There are other times when the Holy Spirit needs to tell it like it is, convicting us and leading us away from sin and into truth.

A few years ago, I wrestled with my anger toward a family member. Fuming, I watched the fire in the fireplace and tried to figure out what I should do. As I sat there, the fire burned down, while the embers remained hot and orange. Eventually, I needed to make a decision about the fire. Should I get up and stir the embers and add another log? Or let the fire burn out? In an instant, I felt the Holy Spirit's gentle voice lead me to the right path: *Let the fire in your heart burn out. Do not add another log to the fire in this relationship. Don't fuel the fight. Let it go!*

The gentle voice was the opposite of everything I felt, which is one reason I knew it was the Holy Spirit. *I* wanted to fan the fire and pursue the fight, but this gentle prompting gave me the spiritual insight I needed. *"Keep quiet and let it go!"* Ultimately, this important but small decision was essential in uniting the family. By following the Spirit's leading, I was free and at peace. Even years later, I know God rescued me from myself.

When our ears tune in to the voice of the Holy Spirit, we quickly see that He is always speaking. Often I hear phrases like, *"Don't say that." "This is gossip." "You don't need that."* Even when it's gentle, it's hard to argue with the voice of God, and often, I'm able to discern the voice of the Holy Spirit because the prompting goes against everything my flesh so badly wants to indulge.

~~~~~~

I remember early one morning, as a young mother, standing in the kitchen, getting ready for the day. I could hear my son, Willis's, little feet hit the floor as he slowly made his way downstairs. The sound of his footie pajamas sliding made me so happy because I knew that he was coming to me for his early-morning hug. I listened and happily waited to greet him. Greeting and hugging each of my children was a highlight of my day. In the morning, everyone was rested and happy. It was a new day. Too early for meltdowns and disobedience, the early-morning hours were when we shined. When I heard Willis's feet hit the final stair, I was ready. To my surprise, instead of coming through the kitchen, as he always did, he took a new route, through the dining room into the den to see his sisters.

For some reason, this little scene filled me with disappointment. I was expectantly waiting for him, but Willis passed me by not even noticing that I was waiting for my morning hug. He was more interested in his sisters.

As I processed the scene, I felt the Holy Spirit whisper, *"Lisa, this is how I feel when you are too busy to greet me first thing in the morning. I look forward to being with you."* That morning, the Holy Spirit helped me to see that the God of the universe anticipates and enjoys meeting with me. The time I spend with Him in the morning praying, reading, talking, and journaling matters to Him. He waits for me to wake up and meet with Him. And when I bypass Him for other things, He notices. This insight was both exciting and convicting. I've never forgotten this picture, and it has served as a continual reminder that how I choose to spend the first moments of my day matters to God.

Recently, the Holy Spirit began nudging me about my online

news consumption. I didn't listen right away, but little by little, I noticed just how much I opened my computer to check the headlines. Whenever I had three to five minutes, I found myself hopping online to read the news. The world news is so depressing! Slowly, I acknowledged the voice of the Holy Spirit and pulled back on reading the news. Almost immediately, I felt my head clear and I had more capability to think, pray, and hear the voice of the Holy Spirit. While initially I resisted, as I surrendered to the Holy Spirit, I saw that this conviction wasn't to hurt me but to give me even more life. Now I try to check the news only once or twice a day, and as a result I have had a quieter mind.

The psalmist asked the Lord, "Point out anything in me that offends you, and lead me along the path of everlasting life" (Psalm 139:24). He was asking the Holy Spirit to make him aware of anything that was offensive to God. When we are tuned in to the Holy Spirit and confront the things that offend Him, we become free from the obstacles separating us from God and free to joyfully skip down the right path.

One thing I love about the Lord is how patient He is with us. For years, my daughter heard the voice of the Holy Spirit telling her to stop watching TV. She would give it up for seasons here and there, but she couldn't ever fully let it go and always found herself back in a cyclical pattern of watching anything and everything. This push and pull went on for several years, until one day, she heard the voice tell her very clearly and specifically to stop watching certain shows. Since it wasn't cold turkey, it felt more manageable, so she reluctantly obliged, and shows she once felt she "couldn't live without" very quickly became shows she didn't miss at all.

Little by little, the Holy Spirit convicted her of nearly every show she was watching. But rather than feel as though she was missing out, she quickly saw how much more time in her life she had been given—time to focus on more important things than the latest reality show. She will tell you now that her playlist is mainly capped at *Fixer Upper* and the Hallmark show *When Calls the Heart*, based on the Christian fiction novel by Janette Oke.

Should my daughter have listened to the voice of the Holy Spirit years ago? Yes. Had she, who knows what God could have done with the hours she'd wasted zoning out in front of a screen. But that's what I love about the Holy Spirit: He's patient and He doesn't stop nudging.

Other times, the voice of conviction is loud and clear. There's no process, no transition, just a clear and direct "*Stop! This is not pleasing to Me.*" When we hear that voice, we can't mess around. Be quick to heed the voice of God and obey.

Though we all get our nudges, it's important not to compare your convictions with those of others around you. Is news or is all TV bad for us? Not necessarily. My husband was the CEO of a major television network for many years, and my father-in-law hosts *The 700 Club*, the longest-running television show in history with the same host, so I'm not allowed to say all TV is bad! What's important is that your ears are tuned in to hear what and how the Holy Spirit is speaking to you.

At the same time, we need to be more focused on our own convictions than on trying to "convict" those around us. Yes, there is a time for godly confrontation, but I've found it's best to leave the convicting up to the Holy Spirit and pray that eventually the person will listen.

My success with the conviction of the Holy Spirit comes when I hear the gentle voice and then do what He is saying. It's not a one-way street—I have to participate with the Lord. He shows me, and I respond. The Holy Spirit's conviction doesn't change my life if I don't follow through with it. In my favorite partnership, we work together toward success and freedom.

The Voice That Condemns

On the other hand, there is the voice of condemnation—and it's a voice that hurts. It is harsh and full of lies. It speaks words like, "*You are so pathetic.*" "*You are the worst mother* [or person or teacher]." "*You'll never be able to do it.*" "*No one cares about what you think or say.*" "*How could you be so stupid?*" Condemnation taunts and cripples us. It tears us down, plagues us with insecurity, robs us of confidence in who God is and who we are in God. Condemnation steals, kills, and destroys us. Remind you of someone? Condemnation is the voice of the accuser. This voice lies and is not to be believed.

Unfortunately, many women listen to condemnation and believe every word. We wear the heaviness of these words like a lead jacket, weighing us down until we can't get up. "Stay alert!" Peter warned. "Watch out for your great enemy, the devil. He prowls around like a roaring lion, looking for someone to devour" (1 Peter 5:8). Our enemy is real, and he is looking to destroy us with condemnation. Yet, even when we know it's the enemy prowling around, seeking to take us out, why do we allow ourselves to believe his lies?

There is an ongoing battle for our minds, and Satan is sneaky. How quickly our thoughts give way to deceiving us, flooding our minds with lies. We can be praising and worshipping God one minute and then thirty seconds later allow condemning thoughts to creep in and remind us of our failures. Even in church, the accuser never stops.

Judgment Versus Discernment

"Truly, you put them on a slippery path and send them sliding over the cliff to destruction," we read in Psalms (73:18 NLT). As a mother, one of my prayers for my children has been that God would help us to recognize God-given friends, girlfriends, and boyfriends, as well as any friends they should avoid. Most of the time they brought home wonderful friends, but there were some challenging moments with this prayer.

As the children grew older, we often discussed friends by using the word picture *green light*, *yellow light*, and *red light*. This was not a children's game, but a way for me to talk to my children about their friends. This didn't happen very often, but when there was a red-light friend, these descriptions served me well.

The first time I used this image was when Willis was a teenager. At a traffic light, he asked me, "Mom, what do you think about Mary?" *Not much* was my first thought, but I responded with an evasive and, I believe, God-inspired answer. "Willis, do you see this traffic light? Now it is red and we are stopped; soon it will be green and we will go. When it is yellow, we proceed with caution. When I see Mary, I see a yellow light. Please proceed with caution."

Truthfully, I saw a red light. He was young, and this was a harmless relationship. To my great relief, within weeks, that little romance ended and he went on with his happy life. Girlfriends were never a big part of Willis's life, until he found his green light—his wife, Caitlin. Willis and Caitlin met when he was twenty-four. A UVA graduate went to Los Angeles, hoping to find fame and fortune, and first he found his wife. (He is still working on the fame and fortune part.) Willis brought her to meet the family one New Year's Eve, and as we were introduced, my eyes filled with tears. Without even thinking about it, I had a deep sense that God had brought Caitlin to Willis and to our family. The tears were an unsolicited response to my sensing God's answers to our prayers for our children. I was surprised by my unprovoked tears, and felt relieved that the Lord was working in Willis's life—even in LA.

Occasionally, the children would bring home friends who alerted me. Sometimes I was being totally judgmental, and other times God was warning us. I continued to use the stoplight illustration to help me understand those feelings and would pray, "Lord, please give me a wise and discerning heart." The expression "yellow light" became a way for me to caution the children.

The Cambridge English dictionary defines *discernment* this way: "The ability to judge people and things well"; another definition is "a perception in the absence of judgment to obtain spiritual direction and understanding." Discernment is a gift from the Holy Spirit, included as one of the spiritual gifts in 1 Corinthians 12:10.

In 1 Kings 3:9 (NIV) Solomon prayed for discernment. "So give your servant a discerning heart to govern your people and to distinguish between right and wrong."

I see this demonstrated today when I have a conflict with the concepts of judgment and discernment. For example, say you're out with friends who want to watch a movie, and you're not sure whether to watch it too. If the movie is a film you've been dying to see but you get a little check in your spirit that watching it isn't the best way you could be spending your time right now, that's probably the voice of the Holy Spirit giving you a boost of discernment. You probably shouldn't go with them to the movie.

If, on the other hand, your friends suggest watching a movie you think is really annoying, and you cannot understand how anyone in their right mind would sit through this chaos, it's probably judgment. You don't have to watch the movie, of course, but you're probably not hearing the discerning voice of the Holy Spirit.

These are two slippery paths. It is important to distinguish between discernment and judgment. *Am I being judgmental, or discerning?* When I ask myself this question, it is the time for me to pray through the concerns and the warnings I feel in my spirit.

The second slippery path is tricky: there is a dangerous

temptation to ignore my God-given discernment because I fear I am being judgy. Be very careful here.

Discernment comes from God's insights, warnings, guidance, and teaching. This gift comes from a place of love and caution. We need to recognize these distinct differences. Being judgmental can lead us to believe a lie. It is deceptive and destructive, and it can be hateful. Discernment is a God-given gift, and when we use it, discernment protects us and strengthens our Christian walk.

Jesus was clear when He spoke about judgment: "Do not judge others, and you will not be judged. For you will be treated as you treat others. The standard you use in judging is the standard by which you will be judged" (Matthew 7:1–2). This teaching seems so clear about the power of judgment. However, sometimes the gift of discernment seems so similar that we run the risk of throwing it out because we fear we are being judgmental. The accuser's voice comes in, condemns us, and keeps us from seeing God's truth.

Fortunately, God was faithful, and little by little, I grew to distinguish the gift of discernment from the sin of judging. Being judgmental is a sin but being discerning is wise because discernment is from God. Discernment shines light and truth on situations. Just like a stoplight, these truths are short and sweet: *Stop. Proceed with caution. Go.* Judgmental thoughts are often unkind or untrue—for example, *I can't stand the way she laughs.* They can be mean-spirited, full of pride, and hurtful.

Following are some steps to help determine if you are discerning or judging:

1. *Pray that God would give you clarity.* He will show you whether to keep praying for greater compassion or understanding, or if you need to minimize your contact.
2. *Make sure your thoughts and actions line up with the Bible.* Sometimes situations are simpler than we think. Other

times they might be more complicated, but God won't contradict His Word.

3. *Find a trusted friend who can pray with you* for clarity in the situation.

4. *Wait it out.* If you're in a situation or relationship and you don't think you're hearing anything from God, stay the course. He'll make it clear when and if it's time to move on.

Usually, when I am being straight-up judgmental, I'm not worried about being judgmental. I'm just judging! The fact that I have to ask the question at all probably indicates some degree of discernment. When I sense a God-given warning that feels like a "Proceed with caution," I pay attention and pray. I stay alert and ask the Holy Spirit to guide me and help me see people through the eyes of Jesus.

The most important part of this chapter is to encourage you not to sacrifice discernment and ignore the voice of the Holy Spirit because you are afraid of being judgmental. This is so easy to do, and it dismisses the power of discernment. Don't forget that God gives us the gift of discernment for our protection. Keep asking the Holy Spirit to help you see the difference.

Fighting the Battle for Our Minds

There is a battle for our minds, and we need to arm ourselves against condemnation and judgment. We also need a strategy so that we can wage war with "a sound mind" (2 Timothy 1:7 NKJV).

The first way we fight is with the Word of God. "The word of God is alive and powerful. It is sharper than the sharpest two-edged sword" (Hebrews 4:12). God's Word is filled with truth and meaning. When we stand on the Word of God and use Scripture as our weapon, nothing can overcome us. I love that there is literally a verse for every situation you may be facing, and when it comes to our thoughts, Scripture is full of gems to pray:

- "Thank You that though I am human, I don't wage war as humans do. Rather than leave me to fight with worldly weapons, You equip me with Your mighty weapons to knock down strongholds of human reasoning and destroy every false argument. Help me to capture every rebellious thought and make it obedient to Christ." (2 Corinthians 10:3–5)
- "May I not be conformed to the pattern of this world, but transform me by the renewing of my mind." (Romans 12:2)
- "Thank You that You have not given us a spirit of fear, but of power and of love and of a sound mind. Come into my mind and make it sound. Take my fears and doubts, and in You may my mind be steady and secure." (2 Timothy 1:7)
- "Lord, in all things, may I set my mind on the things of You, not on the things of this world. I surrender my thoughts that give way to the world, and ask You to help me fix my mind on You." (Colossians 3:2)

If Satan is waging war on our minds, looking to rob us every chance he gets, we need to be armed and ready to fight with prayer. Praying the above scriptures is a great place to start. There is also so much power in the spoken word. In praying Scripture, we can disagree with the voice of the accuser, openly declare who God is, and confidently speak what His Word says.

Years ago, I participated in Beth Moore's Bible study *Believing God*. In it, she talks about one strategy for combatting the negative thoughts and words that overcome us. When those thoughts begin to take root, she literally puts her hand on her head, palm open, and symbolically pushes the thoughts away from her mind, saying out loud, "I do not receive that. I do not receive that."

I find so much strength in making a physical motion, as if to literally drive away condemnation and judgment from my mind. That doubt, shame, accusation, insecurity slowly creeping in? Push it away through prayer. "In the name of Jesus, I will not receive that. I refuse to allow this to take hold of my mind."

The third way we can fight in the battle of our minds is through praise. As we've already touched on in chapter 8, there is power in singing praises to the Lord.

I like the words from the popular and powerful worship anthem "Surrounded." I heard my daughter singing it one day in the kitchen and my question to her was, "How *do* you fight your battles?" She continued to sing "This is how I fight my battles" and answered "With praise!"

Don't forget we can fight our battles by thanking God for His many blessings.

Recently, I've come to love the Passion Translation (TPT) of the Bible. To keep things fresh, I try to change up the translations I read. If I read only one translation, it can become too familiar, and I don't give it my full attention. Look at Psalm 149 from the Passion Translation:

> Hallelujah! Praise the Lord!
> It's time to sing to God a brand-new song. . . .
> God's high and holy praises fill [his godly lovers'] mouths,
> *for their shouted praises are their weapons of war!*
> These warring weapons will bring vengeance
> on every opposing force and every resistant power—
> to bind kings with chains and rulers with iron shackles.
> Praise-filled warriors will enforce
> the judgment-doom decreed against their enemies.
> This is the glorious honor he gives to all his godly lovers.
> Hallelujah! Praise the Lord! (emphasis added)

"Their shouted praises are their weapons of war!" Think about it—our shouted praise becomes a weapon of war. How powerful!

When it comes to a battle in my mind, another "go-to" passage is 2 Chronicles 20, where Jehoshaphat defeated Moab and Ammon. A messenger of the Lord came to Jehoshaphat and said:

> "Do not be afraid or discouraged because of this vast army. For the battle is not yours, but God's. . . . You will not have to fight this battle. Take up your positions; stand firm and see the deliverance the Lord will give you, Judah and Jerusalem. Do not be afraid; do not be discouraged. Go out to face them tomorrow, and the LORD will be with you." (vv. 15, 17 NIV)

When Jehoshaphat heard this, he fell to the ground and worshipped the Lord. The next day, early in the morning, Jehoshaphat appointed men to sing praises to God, going out ahead of the army, declaring, "Give thanks to the LORD, for his love endures forever" (v. 21 NIV). And as they praised the Lord, He brought the victory. After the battle, it took them three days to collect all the plunder, and as soon as they had scooped up as much plunder as they could carry, they met together and praised the Lord once again, for His deliverance.

Before, during, and after the battle, Jehoshaphat and his men praised God. As their lips were filled with the praises of the Lord, they watched in awe as the Lord surrounded them, fought for them, and brought deliverance on all sides. Praise is a powerful weapon. "Shout unto God with a voice of triumph" (Psalm 47:1 KJV), and as His praises fill your lips, let your mind be fixated on who God is, His power and His glory. And as your praises grow, stand firm, and see the deliverance the Lord will give you, as the voice of the accuser shrinks away.

The battle for our minds is never-ending, and in this war—to know the difference between conviction and condemnation and discernment and judgment—we need the tools of the Holy Spirit. The gentle voice of the Holy Spirit brings truth, life, answers, and freedom. This voice adds to you and fortifies you.

The condemning voice of Satan is filled with lies, harsh words, and destruction. It destroys and tears you down. It will also squash the life and peace given to you by the Holy Spirit. Jesus explained it this way: "The thief's purpose is to steal and kill and destroy. My purpose is to give them a rich and satisfying life" (John 10:10).

I'm not going to stand back and watch anyone steal from, kill, and destroy me.

Between these two teachings, I am motivated to listen and respond to the leading of the gentle voice of God and be on guard so that the "thief" cannot steal anything from me.

Chapter 11

〜〜〜

The Path of God for You

"This is what the LORD says—your Redeemer, the Holy One of Israel: 'I am the LORD your God, who teaches you what is good for you and leads you along the paths you should follow'" (Isaiah 48:17). Every one of us has a God-given path. While each experience is different, each path is uniquely ours. The journey will be rocky at times and smooth at other times. It is always wise to be ready for all that comes across your path. You can be confident that your path has a destination, that God is with you, that He will never leave you, and that He walks before you, leading you as you travel.

This has been an incredible learning experience for me, and it has been an interesting and exciting path to walk on. I started with one simple path of life, and through reading and searching, I discovered the truth that God has prepared a unique path for each one of us. "Who are those who fear the LORD?" the psalmist wrote. "He will show them the path they should choose" (Psalm 25:12). What a wonderful statement! Simple to understand but difficult to follow.

Thankfully, the Bible gives us very specific directions to navigate these paths:

1. Ask God. (Matthew 7:7; James 4:2)
2. Partner and participate. (John 2:5–8; Matthew 14:16–21)
3. Seek God with all your heart. (Jeremiah 29:11–13; Matthew 6:21, 33)
4. In everything give thanks. (Ephesians 5:20)

As studied in chapter 4, asking God is so basic to life. We are encouraged not only to ask God but also to partner and participate with Him.

Praise turns our hearts and minds from ourselves to the miracle-working power of God. It sets our hearts free to trust God and helps us to remember His faithfulness to us in the past. Thanks and praise establish and remind us that our God is a God who has a plan, purpose, and path for each one of us. We will find it because He will show us the way.

Even though our stories will be different, these four concepts will apply to all of us and help us find our paths, listen to God, and learn to trust Him step-by-step.

When I first started my journey, "the path of life" was the only path that I was aware of in the Bible. This path is probably the most important, and I never thought about any of the others. As life moved on, however, I began to find and treasure other paths that God had prepared. Once I began to look for more throughout the Bible, I found so many. I have included scriptures concerning these paths in the appendix.

Some of the first words I heard after my commitment to Christ, "God has a plan for your life. But that doesn't mean that you will find it or fulfill it," directed me to be diligent in the search for my God-ordained path. This was both a promise—God has a plan—and a threat—you may not succeed. It motivated me.

I have written about the power of the acronym ASK: **A**sk and it shall be given to you. **S**eek and you will find. **K**nock and the door will be opened to you. These words are so clear in establishing the partnership we have with the Lord. Our faith doesn't depend only on us: Are we good enough? Have we worked hard enough? Do we love God enough? We can't get to heaven by trying extra hard to be "better." Conversely, our relationship with Christ doesn't depend only on Him. The teaching to ask establishes the *partnership* we have with the Lord.

In the New Testament, we read about Jesus asking people to participate with Him in His miracles. Often, He didn't just do a miracle; He asked the people around Him to get involved, to participate, to be in partnership with Him.

The God Who Asks

Jesus' first recorded miracle was at a wedding in Cana of Galilee. There, He turned water into wine, a fine wine. There was a need at the wedding: the family had no wine for the celebration. Mary approached Jesus and asked for help. Like a good mother, Mary took charge of the situation to make sure things were done properly. The servants listened and responded.

> [Jesus'] mother told the servants, "Do whatever he tells you."
>
> Standing nearby were six stone water jars, used for Jewish ceremonial washing. Each could hold twenty to thirty gallons. Jesus told the servants, "Fill the jars with water." When the jars had been filled, he said, "Now dip some out, and take it to the master of ceremonies." So the servants followed his instructions. (John 2:5–8)

When the servants participated with Jesus and did as He had instructed, they saw a miracle. The people obeyed, and Jesus did the heavy lifting. He did the miraculous.

~~~~~~~

The feeding of the five thousand is one of my favorite miracles. All four Gospels include this story (Matthew 14:13–21; Mark 6:30–44; Luke 9:10–17; John 6:1–15). Some say that it may have happened more than once. I love this miracle because of its simplicity and power.

The people had gathered and were listening to Jesus' teaching. After a while, they became hungry, but there was not enough food to feed so many. Jesus asked His disciples what food they had. They told Him that there was a boy who had five loaves of bread and some fish (John 6:9). You can be sure that the boy's mother had carefully packed his meal before he left to follow Jesus, and now Jesus was asking the boy to give it all to Him. The boy gave Jesus everything he had. And Jesus took it all. He didn't say, "You are a young lad and need your strength, so let's share this." No, Jesus probably said, "Thank you!" Here's one account:

> But Jesus said to them, "They do not need to go away. You give them something to eat."
>
> And they said to Him, "We have here only five loaves and two fish."
>
> He said, "Bring them here to Me." Then He commanded the multitudes to sit down on the grass. And He took the five loaves and the two fish, and looking up to heaven, He blessed and broke and gave the loaves to the disciples; and the disciples gave to the multitudes. So they all ate and were filled, and they took up twelve baskets full of the fragments that remained. Now those who had eaten were about five thousand men, besides women and children. (Matthew 14:16–21 NKJV)

The disciples complained about hungry people and Jesus said, "You feed them." Again, He gave them a job, and they were invited into the miracle. Jesus took the loaves and the fish that the boy had given to Him, looked to heaven, and blessed them. The disciples and a boy shared and worked in this miracle. They were in partnership with Jesus to feed the people.

I used to think that when Jesus worked a miracle, He just did the miracle. But now I have learned how important it is for us not to simply be spectators but to be ready for Jesus to give us an assignment. "Do what He tells you to do." "You feed them," He told the disciples.

This isn't to say that Jesus won't work His miracles without us; He can do anything without us. He is God Almighty. Sometimes He invites us into His miraculous world so that we can witness it for ourselves and see His great work.

He wants us to be in partnership with Him too. The boy shared the food; Jesus took it, blessed it, and multiplied it so that everyone had more than enough to eat. The disciples distributed it and then gathered the leftovers. There were leftovers!

Like the disciples and the crowd listening to Jesus, we have assignments from Jesus too. He may ask us to give Him our time, share our gifts, donate our money, offer our ideas, and more. When we know that He has asked us, that is the time for us to act.

As we begin to give what He asks of us, our hearts become more attuned to God's work. In this process, we may glimpse His power and presence. Without a doubt, we will not be deprived but will benefit when we share. He doesn't need anything from us, but we need to let go and learn to trust Him with the outcome. Everything we have is from God; why do we hold on?

The people watched the miracle of the loaves and fish, they saw the boy give the bread and fish to Jesus, and they witnessed a miracle when Jesus multiplied what was offered. The Bible is clear: when we release our things to God, He brings us a return that is *infinitely more than we might ask or think* (Ephesians 3:20). Often, even when I know what God can and will do, I still want to hold on and be satisfied with my way instead of moving into the place of miracles and blessing.

The God Who Gives

"He will show [those who fear him] the path they should choose. They will live in prosperity, and their children will inherit the land. The LORD is a friend to those who fear him" (Psalm 25:12–14). If someone asked me to describe God, I would start with the tried and true: faithful, loving, Lord, Creator, and many more. It wouldn't take me too long before I moved in other words: *generous*, *extravagant*, and *daring*.

One of the great truths that God has taught me over and over again is, "Give and it shall be given unto you." Or put another way, "You cannot outgive God." When I was a young girl and sent to church, my parents often gave me a quarter for the offering plate. On my way to the church, I would buy a ten-cent pack of gum and feel that God was so lucky to get the change. After all, I could have spent the whole thing and God could have gotten nothing. I knew nothing about the extravagance of God, and this is one of the most exciting lessons to learn.

Before we were married, Tim worked hard and saved about $1,000. We thought this money could pay for our honeymoon, our security deposit, our first month's rent on an apartment, and everything else we needed. *Thank You, Lord*, was the song on my heart. However, the January before we were married, Tim called me in Denver and told me that he felt that the Lord was asking him to give the money away. We weren't married, it was his money, and I didn't think that I should say anything sweet, like, "Are you crazy?" My mother was not at all impressed that her daughter was about to marry someone who appeared to be young and irresponsible. He gave the money away and I was okay with it. I knew it was not my job to tell Tim what God was saying to him. I had to trust the Lord and Tim with this idea.

About a week later, a friend, Wayne Campbell, stopped Tim at CBN and asked him where we were going on our honeymoon. Our wedding was in April, this was February, and we hadn't finalized our plans. Where we *wanted* to go and where we could *afford* to go were two different things. After all, we had to pay to get from our wedding in Denver back to our new home in Virginia. Maybe that trip would be our honeymoon? Tim told Wayne that we weren't sure what we were doing for our honeymoon.

Wayne continued, "I own a travel agency in Canada. If you and Lisa can get to Montreal, I will give you two airline tickets to anywhere in the world you would like to go."

Tim almost fell over. "Anywhere? Free?"

"Yes!" was the answer.

You can imagine our joy as we began to plan our honeymoon. Greece and the Greek Islands were our final destination. A honeymoon trip from Colorado to Virginia would have been wonderful, but heading off to Greece was beyond a dream come true.

My sweet mother, who had been so concerned about Tim and his seemingly reckless faith, promptly reevaluated her own giving to the Lord. Mom walked closely with God. She knew the teachings about God's generosity, but she had started a business and she had business loans. She didn't think that she could give of her tithes and offerings until she got out of debt. As she watched what God had done in our lives, how He had opened the windows of heaven and poured out a blessing so great that we couldn't contain it (Malachi 3:10), Mom began to give to the Lord too. To her joy and delight, as she gave to the Lord, He blessed and prospered her business.

What the Lord gives back to us isn't always money; it can be many other blessings: health, family, friendships, peace, and joy. There are blessings that money can't buy. God is the source of these too.

"The love of money is the root of all evil," says 1 Timothy 6:10. It doesn't say that money is the root of all evil, but the love of money is. We are to love and worship God and not let money, or the lack of it, own us. "Possessed by our possessions" is what I call it.

The steps Tim took before we received this honeymoon blessing are important. He prayed and thanked God for this money. God spoke to Tim about the money. Tim heard God, trusted Him, and then obeyed Him by giving the money to the Lord's work.

"Trust and Obey" is an old song, and those words are foundational to any successful Christian walk. The steps are clear, but actually taking them is a challenge. God wants us to give of ourselves, to trust Him with our giving of both time and financial resources and then to watch Him work in our lives. "Give, and it will be given to you. A good measure, pressed down, shaken together and running over, will be poured into your lap" (Luke 6:38 NIV).

Trust and Obey

"Trust and Obey," the old gospel hymn I mentioned, was written by John H. Sammis in 1887. The chorus goes like this:

> Trust and obey, for there's no other way
> to be happy in Jesus, but to trust and obey.

Yes, this is another song that has helped define my life. Through the opportunities God gives to trust Him and follow His direction, not only will we grow in our faith and understanding of God, but we will also have more opportunities to trust and obey.

Laura, my oldest child, was a gift from God. Not only was she kind, beautiful, and sweet; she was also much smarter than me, even at a very young age. As she learned her letters and the sounds of each one, she earnestly asked me if the letter *W* started with a *D* ("double u"). When she learned her odd and even numbers, she wanted to know if infinity was odd or even? I don't think like that, but I loved having a child stretch my mind in this way.

Each child started preschool, three days a week, at age four. Because I had so many children at home, I felt like my house was a preschool and didn't feel the need for more.

Laura was so excited to finally enter the school world, and she thrived. By the time she was ready to start first grade, Tim wanted us to look at a different school, one with a stronger academic reputation, because he felt that Laura needed more of a challenge. I loved the security of a small Christian school, a school that loved and nurtured Laura. I felt safe there and didn't want to leave it.

Tim was certain that we needed to look into other opportunities, and we did, although I was reluctant. Laura was given a spot in the first-grade class. We had until April 17 to accept her place. Tim had no doubt about her going, and I held on to the acceptance as long as I could, hoping he would change his mind. The new school was a great school, and this was a wonderful opportunity for Laura, but I was afraid. I wanted to hold on to what was comfortable for us.

As the days passed, Tim didn't change his mind. I knew that after we prayed together about this, talked about the benefits and challenges, prayed again, if we still disagreed, the final decision would be Tim's. I trusted God to speak to Tim when my words didn't change his mind. God had Tim's heart, and I knew God could lead Tim to the right decision.

Tim and God were unwavering on Laura going to the new school. I waited until Friday, the last day to hand-deliver her acceptance, and I drove to the school. Entering the campus, I noticed there were no cars in the lot, no students on the fields; the school was empty, and the school was closed. I drove to the door, sat in my car, and wondered why no one was there. *Why did I wait so long to turn this in?* I was so upset with myself, and now I wasn't even able to turn in her acceptance.

Seemingly out of nowhere, a man came to my car and asked if he could help me. I showed him the envelope and told him why I was there. He "happened" to have a key to the school and was happy to deliver our letter to the admissions director's desk. He informed me that the school was closed because it was Good Friday!

The Lord works in mysterious ways. With all my fears and uncertainty about the new school, in just five minutes of being at the closed school on Good Friday, having a stranger come to answer my prayers gave me the confidence that God was with us and in our decision to send Laura there. Immediately, I was comforted because I sensed that God had provided this new step on our path.

Once again, I learned to trust God, trust Tim, and follow the plans that the Lord was showing us. Laura stayed for all twelve years, followed by the rest of the children. The school became an important part of our family life, and I still thank God for guiding us there.

The Power of Praise and Thanksgiving

Another basic and important lesson on the path of life is that we must be diligent to give thanks and praise in everything: "Be filled with the Holy Spirit. . . . And you will always give thanks for everything to God the Father in the name of our Lord Jesus Christ" (Ephesians 5:18, 20).

The Power in Praise by Merlin Carothers is the first Christian book I read. I learned the foundational teachings about giving thanks to God for everything! By doing this, we not only learn more about Him, but we also learn to trust Him because He is trustworthy. As we give thanks and praise, the challenges of our lives find answers. Often our perspective changes. For things that once seemed so impossible, praise can give us peace.

The decision to trust God builds our confidence in His faithfulness and miracle-working power. "And we know that God causes everything to work together for the good of those who love God and are called according to his purpose for them" (Romans 8:28). God will use *everything* in our lives to teach us, correct us, humble us, and use us. If we believe the Bible, we can believe this promise too.

God does the miracles. He works it out. He is God Almighty. There is nothing out of His reach or His power. Knowing this helps us thank God and confidently trust His ways.

We have already learned in "Prayers for the Path" and "The Path of Joy" some very specific instructions. "Always be joyful. Keep on praying. No matter what happens, always be thankful, for this is God's will for you who belong to Christ" (1 Thessalonians 5:16–18 TLB). Or we can say it another way: God's will for you is to choose joy, pray continually, and always, always be thankful.

These are imperative words—direct, concise, and to the point. They are like a recipe to help us trust God: choose joy; pray all the time; always give thanks. God wants His best for us. He knows exactly what His best is and how we can receive it. Thanks and praise establish our trust, our confidence, and our gratitude.

The challenge to thank God in everything has been educational, and it takes faith. One day I had two flat tires. They didn't happen at the same time. We discovered the first flat tire in the church parking lot and changed it. We noticed the second one in our driveway and had to call for help because I didn't have two spares. I kept my frustrations under control and said, "Thank You, Lord, for these two flat tires! What a memorable day for my children and me." This may seem ridiculous to you, but when I stepped out and thanked God, it defused my emotions and kept me in balance instead of yelling at the children or at God.

There are far more difficult situations when we are challenged to thank God. When I practice in the smaller ones, I learn how to keep thanking and praising God, and I am ready for other opportunities to watch Him work through my thanks and praise. In everything give Him thanks, and let Him work through you and through your circumstances.

Some of the benefits of thanking God in all things come from keeping our eyes on the Lord and inviting Him into our challenges. He becomes an important partner in how I navigate my life. Problems don't overwhelm me as easily.

The path of praise is one that I have learned to walk throughout the years, and on this path I have felt God's comfort, confidence in His plan, and the thrill of a great adventure.

The process of giving thanks prepares us for the next step—which is to seek Him, listen, and obey His voice.

Seek

Even after many years, I still discover new steps on the path. One such step is learning about the significance of seeking God. Scripture consistently challenges us to seek Him. I am experienced and comfortable in my faith. I know what to do and how to pray, and I have an idea of what to expect. Often, I don't feel the need to press in more, to earnestly seek the Lord, because I am too comfortable with my faith. But when I do, I find that God has much more for me!

Many great verses encourage us to seek God, and most of them tell us to seek Him with all our hearts. Seeking God places us in an important partnership with Him. When we seek Him, He will reveal His plans and promises to us.

> "For I know the plans I have for you," declares the LORD, "plans to prosper you and not to harm you, plans to give you hope and a future. Then you will call on me and come to me and I will listen to you. You will seek me and find me when you seek me with all your heart." (Jeremiah 29:11–13 NIV)

Does it say *if* we seek the Lord, He will reveal His plans for us and give us a hope and a future? No, it clearly says, "You will seek me and find me when you seek me with all your heart."

Here are some other places that encourage us to seek God with our "hearts."

- Seek the LORD your God, and you will find Him if you seek Him with all of your heart and with all of your soul. (Deuteronomy 4:29 NKJV)
- I seek you with all of my heart; do not let me stray from your commands. (Psalm 119:10 NIV)
- Seek first the kingdom of God. . . . For where your treasure is, there your heart will be also. (Matthew 6:33, 21 NKJV)

Seeking God is not simply asking a question or reading a passage. Seeking God with all of our hearts is a full commitment. It involves all that we have and all that we are. It is a full-court press, a single-minded effort to seek God. Distractions are not welcomed.

Some of the biblical results of seeking God are clear. When we seek, we will find. The Lord is good to those who seek; seek the kingdom and all the other things you need will be added to you.

Of course, I don't know the specific plans the Lord has for you. He knows! But I do know that we can count on these things as we open our road map—God's Word—and look toward Him.

There is so much to discover in the Bible, as it is filled with many insights on the path of life. God said, through the prophet Isaiah, "I am the LORD, your God, who teaches you what is good for you and leads you along the paths you should follow" (Isaiah 48:17).

God is speaking to us with great assurance of His leadership and lordship. He is the Lord who teaches us and guides us. We are encouraged to ask Him to reveal His best path to us. He teaches us to partner and participate with Him. We are never alone in struggling to find the way; He is available at all times to go with us on this journey.

We carry with us the great promise that when we seek with all of our hearts, we will find Him. To top it off, another power surge comes after we seek Him and then give thanks for everything. Thank Him for the new day, your loved ones, His faithfulness to you in every challenge, and joy. He has great plans, purposes, and promises for all of us. When we seek Him, be encouraged that we will find those things!

Knowing all this, I am once again led back to the words of Psalm 16:11, words that have supported me with strength, comfort, and motivation for the majority of my adult life: "You will make known to me the path of life; In Your presence is fullness of joy; In Your right hand there are pleasures forever" (NASB).

Daily, I look to follow God's path. On His path, I will enter

His presence and be filled with joy. His joy is my strength. And I can discover God's pleasures every day of my life and into eternity.

This promise fills me with excitement and purpose and motivates me to keep walking on His path. I hope and pray it will do the same for you.

Acknowledgments

"I am the Lord your God, who teaches
what is good for you and leads you along
the paths you should follow."
—*Isaiah 48:17*

Thanks to our children and their fabulous families. Your willingness to follow the path of life and teach your children to walk on it brings us great joy. Your advice and insights have been invaluable. We are so proud of all of you.

Thank you to my parents, Babby and David. You walked with me on my first mountain paths. Whether we were walking to school or swim team, you taught me to appreciate the wonder of the amazing clouds, the beauty of the golden aspen leaves, and the joy of walking together. Thank you for showing me the way and teaching me to love the wonder of God's creation that surrounds us.

Thank you to Dede and Pat. You have blazed an amazing trail for all of us to follow. Thank you for your incredible faithfulness and dedication as you steadfastly follow God's incredible path.

All of us are better because of the love and leadership of our parents.

Thank you to my siblings and friends who have listened, prayed, and advised me as we navigated our paths together. Because of you, I discovered the word twalk—a walk where we talk about all the important issues in our lives. You have kept me going, picked me up, and made me laugh on the path.

There are so many others who helped me on this path. The Galilee Women's Bible Study: thank you for listening to me and helping me. Debbie and Pat at Virginia Beach Printing: thank you for your friendship, kindness, and generous help.

As I wrote this book, I often heard the voice of my favorite English teacher, Judy Wilson Grant. You taught me so much through your insistence that I write smarter and better. You gave me a love of writing, and because of you, I went to Sweet Briar College. You shaped my life in many important ways. Thank you!

Thank you, Josie and many others who read and corrected the manuscript. Your wisdom was so helpful.

Jack Hayford and Catherine Marshall have written books that fortified my faith and understanding of the incredible journey of life. Thank you both for your inspiration.

Thank you, Molly Young from CBN. You are a treasured friend and you introduced me to Emanate Books.

Last but not least, thank you to my new friends at Emanate: Joel Kneedler, Janene MacIvor, and Kristen Golden. We met by "accident" or a divine coincidence. You have been fabulous in the ways that you encouraged me and kept me moving on the path. Thank you so much for believing in me and sharing the joy of walking on God's Path of Life.

Thank you all for your prayers, insights, wisdom, love, encouragement, and patience!

I thank God for you.

Thanks be to God for His indescribable gift! (2 Corinthians 9:15 NKJV)

Appendix

Scriptures for the Path

The Path of Life

You will make known to me the path of life;
In Your presence is fullness of joy;
In Your right hand there are pleasures forever. (Psalm 16:11 NASB)

The First Step on the Path

"I am the way, the truth, and the life." (John 14:6)

You are my God. Show me
    what you want me to do,
    and let your gentle Spirit
    lead me in the right path. (Psalm 143:10 CEV)

    He renews my strength.
He guides me along right paths,
    bringing honor to his name. (Psalm 23:3)

The Surprising Path

Your road led through the sea,
> your pathway through the mighty waters—
> a pathway no one knew was there! (Psalm 77:19)

Then Moses raised his hand over the sea, and the LORD opened up a path through the water with a strong east wind. The wind blew all that night, turning the seabed into dry land. (Exodus 14:21)

He made a dry path through the Red Sea,
> and his people went across on foot.
> There we rejoiced in him. (Psalm 66:6)

The Difficult Path

You crown the year with a bountiful harvest;
> even the hard pathways overflow with abundance.
> (Psalm 65:11)

"Then call on me when you are in trouble,
> and I will rescue you." (Psalm 50:15)

Prayers for the Path: Ask God

We are encouraged to pray and ask God for many things as we travel the path. Here are some verses that encourage us in our prayers.

"Ask me and I will tell you remarkable secrets you do not know about things to come." (Jeremiah 33:3)

"You haven't done this before. Ask, using my name, and you will receive, and you will have abundant joy." (John 16:24)

"Ask, and it will be given to you; seek, and you will find; knock, and it will be opened to you." (Matthew 7:7)

Show me the right path, O LORD;
    point out the road for me to follow. (Psalm 25:4)

Point out anything in me that offends you,
    and lead me along the path of everlasting life. (Psalm 139:24)

The Parenting Path

Trust in the LORD with all your heart;
    do not depend on your own understanding.
Seek his will in all you do,
    and he will show you which path to take. (Proverbs 3:5–6)

Direct your children onto the right path,
    and when they are older, they will not leave it. (Proverbs 22:6)

Follow the steps of the good,
    and stay on the paths of the righteous. (Proverbs 2:20)

The godly walk with integrity;
    blessed are their children who follow them. (Proverbs 20:7)

The Path of Change

Who are those who fear the LORD?
    He will show them the path they should choose.
They will live in prosperity,
    and their children will inherit the land.
The LORD is a friend to those who fear him. (Psalm 25:12–14)

To everything there is a season,
A time for every purpose under heaven. (Ecclesiastes 3:1 NKJV)

The Path of Joy

Always be full of joy in the Lord. I say it again—rejoice! Let everyone see that you are considerate in all you do. Remember, the Lord is coming soon. (Philippians 4:4–5)

Satisfy us in the morning with your unfailing love,
    that we may sing for joy to the end of our lives. (Psalm 90:14)

The LORD has anointed me . . .
to bestow on them a crown of beauty
    instead of ashes,
the oil of joy
    instead of mourning,
and a garment of praise
    instead of a spirit of despair." (Isaiah 61:1, 3 NIV)

May the God of hope fill you with all joy and peace as you trust in him, so that you may overflow with hope by the power of the Holy Spirit. (Romans 15:13 NIV)

The Narrow Path

"You can enter God's Kingdom only through the narrow gate. The highway to hell is broad, and its gate is wide for the many who choose that way. But the gateway to life is very narrow and the road is difficult, and only a few ever find it." (Matthew 7:13–14)

For the LORD God is a sun and a safe-covering.
The Lord gives favor and honor.
He holds back nothing good
   from those who walk in the way that is right. (Psalm 84:11)

The human body has many parts, but the many parts make up one whole body. So it is with the body of Christ. Some of us are Jews, some are Gentiles, some are slaves, and some are free. But we have all been baptized into one body by one Spirit, and we all share the same Spirit. (1 Corinthians 12:12–13)

Therefore, since we are surrounded by such a huge crowd of witnesses to the life of faith, let us strip off every weight that slows us down, especially the sin that so easily trips us up. And let us run with endurance the race God has set before us. We do this by keeping our eyes on Jesus, the champion who initiates and perfects our faith. (Hebrews 12:1–2)

Potholes on the Path

If you think you are standing strong, be careful not to fall. (1 Corinthians 10:12)

Those who love your instructions have great peace
and do not stumble. (Psalm 119:165)

My child, don't lose sight of common sense and discernment.
Hang on to them. (Proverbs 3:21)

"Do not judge others, and you will not be judged. For you will be treated as you treat others. The standard you use in judging is the standard by which you will be judged." (Matthew 7:1–2)

Let those with discernment listen carefully. The paths of the LORD are true and right, and righteous people live by walking in them. But in those paths sinners stumble and fall. (Hosea 14:9)

The Path of God for You

This is what the LORD says—your Redeemer, the Holy One of Israel: "I am the LORD your God, who teaches you what is good for you and leads you along the paths you should follow." (Isaiah 48:17)

Who are those who fear the Lord?
He will show them the path they should choose.
They will live in prosperity,
and their children will inherit the land. (Psalm 25:12–13)

You are my God. Show me
what you want me to do,
and let your gentle Spirit
lead me in the right path. (Psalm 143:10 CEV)

The LORD says, "I will guide you along the best pathway
for your life.
I will advise you and watch over you." (Psalm 32:8)

Put your hope in the LORD.
Travel steadily along his path.
He will honor you by giving you the land. (Psalm 37:34)

Other Paths in the Bible

A Dark Path

There is a path before each person that seems right,
but it ends in death. (Proverbs 16:25)

A Wide Path

You provide a broad path for my feet,
so that my ankles do not give way. (Psalm 18:36 NIV)

You have made a wide path for my feet
to keep them from slipping. (Psalm 18:36)

Hope for the Path

Put your hope in the LORD.
Travel steadily along his path.
He will honor you by giving you the land.
You will see the wicked destroyed. (Psalm 37:34)

Muddy Paths

They have stumbled off the ancient highways and walk in muddy
paths. (Jeremiah 18:15)

A Reckless Path

The angel of the LORD asked him, "Why have you beaten your donkey these three times? I have come here to oppose you because your path is a reckless one before me." (Numbers 22:32 NIV)

Winding Paths

In the days of Shamgar son of Anath, in the days of Jael, the highways were abandoned; travelers took to winding paths. (Judges 5:6 NIV)

A Cleared Path

"And you, your lives must be totally obedient to GOD, our personal God, following the life path he has cleared, alert and attentive to everything he has made plain this day." (1 Kings 8:61 THE MESSAGE)

The Best Path

The path of life leads upward for the wise
to keep him from going down to [the grave]. (Proverbs 15:24 TLV)

An Evil Path

Those who obey [God's] laws . . .
do not compromise with evil,
 and they walk only in his paths. (Psalm 119:2–3)

I have refused to walk on any evil path,
 so that I may remain obedient to your word. (Psalm 119:101)

A Wrong Path

Because I consider all your precepts right,
 I hate every wrong path. (Psalm 119:128 NIV)

A Smooth Path

> But for those who are righteous,
>> the way is not steep and rough.
> You are a God who does what is right,
>> and you smooth out the path ahead of them. (Isaiah 26:7)

A Prepared Path

> Righteousness goes before him
>> and prepares the way for his steps. (Psalm 85:13 NIV)

Promises for the Path

Stay on the path that the LORD your God has commanded you to follow. Then you will live long and prosperous lives in the land you are about to enter and occupy. (Deuteronomy 5:33)

"I will lead blind Israel down a new path, guiding them along an unfamiliar way. I will brighten the darkness before them and smooth out the road ahead of them. Yes, I will indeed do these things; I will not forsake them." (Isaiah 42:16)

> I am about to do something new.
>> See, I have already begun! Do you not see it?
> I will make a pathway through the wilderness.
>> I will create rivers in the dry wasteland. (Isaiah 43:19)

Wisdom for the Path

> Seek his will in all you do,
>> and he will show you which path to take. (Proverbs 3:6)

[Wisdom] will guide you down delightful paths;
    all her ways are satisfying.
Wisdom is a tree of life to those who embrace her;
    happy are those who hold her tightly. (Proverbs 3:17–18)

I will teach you wisdom's ways
    and lead you in straight paths.
When you walk, you won't be held back;
    when you run, you won't stumble.
Take hold of my instructions; don't let them go.
    Guard them, for they are the key to life. (Proverbs 4:11–13)

Guidance on the Path

Whether you turn to the right or to the left, your ears will hear a voice behind you, saying, "This is the way; walk in it." (Isaiah 30:21 NIV)

"God's way is perfect. All the Lord's promises prove true. He is a shield for all who look to him for protection. For who is God except the Lord? Who but our God is a solid rock? God is my strong fortress, and he makes my way perfect. He makes me as surefooted as a deer, enabling me to stand on mountain heights. (2 Samuel 22:33–38; 26–37)

Steps on the Path

My steps have held to your paths;
    my feet have not stumbled. (Psalm 17:5 NIV)

Path for the Nation

What joy for the nation whose God is the LORD,
  whose people he has chosen as his inheritance. (Psalm 33:12)

The Path of the Generations

How quickly they turned away from the path of their ancestors, who had walked in obedience to the LORD's commands. (Judges 2:17)

Questions for the Path of Life

Introduction

1. What are the benefits of staying on God's path of life? What happens if you leave it?
2. How do you know you are on the right path?
3. How do you know when you get off the path, and how do you get back on?

Chapter 1: The First Step on the Path

1. What is the first step on the path?
2. What does it mean to surrender?
3. What have you learned about the Trinity?
4. How important are the three parts of the Trinity to your faith?

Chapter 2: The Surprising Path

1. Read Proverbs 3:5–6: "Trust in the LORD with all of your heart. Do not depend on your own understanding. Seek his will in all you do, and he will show you which path to take."
   - What are the three things we are asked to do in this verse?

- What is the promised result?
- Have you seen this work in your life?

2. Read 1 Thessalonians 5:16–18: "Always be joyful. Never stop praying. Be thankful in all circumstances, for this is God's will for you who belong to Christ Jesus."
   - These are instructions to help us live dynamic lives. How would living in this way change your life and your path?

3. Read Isaiah 55:9: "For just as the heavens are higher than the earth, so my ways are higher than your ways and my thoughts higher than your thoughts."
   - According to this verse, why won't we always understand God's path for us? Is this comforting or frustrating?

4. How can we find the path for our life without being distracted by other good choices?

Chapter 3: The Difficult Path

1. Forgiveness and freedom are closely linked in the story this chapter relates. Jesus said, "So if the Son sets you free, you will be free indeed" (John 8:36 NIV). Describe the freedom that you see in this chapter.

2. Babby's (the author's mother) forgiveness unlocked her freedom after Laura's death. How was she able to forgive?

3. Describe a time when your willingness to forgive opened the path for your freedom.

4. Do you see forgiveness as contagious? In Babby's case, forgiveness brought freedom and life to her and those around her. What was the alternative?

5. Psalm 65:11 states that "even the hard pathways overflow with abundance." We know what Babby's hard path was. What kind of abundant life did she receive? Why?

Chapter 4: Prayers for the Path: Ask God

1. What is your takeaway from the story about George Washington Carver?
2. Which verse in this chapter inspires you to ask God?
3. What are the three things Jesus teaches us in Matthew 7:7, summed up in the acronym ASK?
4. The disciples asked Jesus to teach them to pray. Have you ever asked God to teach you how to pray? If so, what did you learn about prayer?
5. Reread Philippians 4:6–7. What are the three guidelines for prayer outlined in these verses? What are the promises given to us about God's peace?

Chapter 5: The Parenting Path: Getting Started

1. The author tells us, "Instead of naming what I saw as 'spoiled, bossy, difficult, and bratty,' I changed my words [about my daughter] to 'determined; knows what she wants; a leader.'" What are some words you should stop using to describe your children? What could you replace them with?
2. Why is it wise not to take either the blame or the credit for your children's behavior?
3. List three qualities of Jesus' character that we should imitate as we parent our children?
4. First Corinthians 13 gives us a great place to begin as we imitate God's ways in parenting. From the famous teaching on love, what are three ways you can imitate God as a parent?
5. Name some important Christian foundations that you want to include in your family.

6. If you have children, how often and when do you pray for them?

7. To quote Thomas Edison, "Our greatest weakness lies in giving up. The most certain way to succeed is always to try just one more time." Is there any area in your life in which you feel like giving up? What can you do to try one more time?

Chapter 6: The Parenting Path: Letting Go

1. What are two of your favorite parenting insights from the book of Proverbs? How can you apply them to your family?

2. If you prayed before you disciplined your child, do you think it would change the way you discipline? If so, how?

3. List some examples of God's discipline for you. How can you imitate His ways?

4. What are the blessings of disciplining with God's wisdom? List some consequences of not disciplining according to God's ways.

5. What is the difference between the way the world wants us to discipline and the wisdom of God's discipline?

6. One of the most dynamic keys to parenting is knowing that God wants to partner with us as parents. He wants us to succeed as parents, and He is always available to help us. What are some ways you have been inspired and/or challenged to partner with God as you parent?

Chapter 7: The Path of Change

Reread Ecclesiastes 3:1–8:

To everything there is a season,

A time for every purpose under heaven:

A time to be born, and a time to die,

A time to plant, and a time to pluck what is planted;

A time to kill, and a time to heal;

A time to break down, and a time to build up;

A time to weep, and a time to laugh;

A time to mourn, and a time to dance;

A time to cast away stones, and a time to gather stones;

A time to embrace, and a time to refrain from embracing;

A time to gain, and a time to lose;

A time to keep, and a time to throw away;

A time to tear, and a time to sew;

A time to keep silence, and a time to speak;

A time to love, and a time to hate;

A time of war, and a time of peace. (NKJV)

1. As you prayerfully read this passage, what changes in life mentioned here stand out to you?
2. How do the changing seasons help us understand and accept the changes in our lives?
3. How might God work through the changes in our churches?
4. The key to successfully navigating change in our lives or in our churches is to stay in close communion with the Lord. How can you invite Him into your struggles, questions, confusion, and/or heartbreak?
5. Trusting God is our choice. What are some new ideas to help you choose to trust God today?
6. What are the challenges of facing a stressful change in the path, such as death, illness, finances, or broken relationships? How can we see God in these times?

Chapter 8: The Path of Joy

1. Psalm 16:11 clearly states, "In Your presence is fullness of joy" (NKJV). What does it mean for you to be in the presence of God?
2. Feelings are fickle. What are some of the things in your life that can influence how you feel, both positively and negatively?
3. God promises us that He will never leave us nor forsake us. How does this truth give you strength and comfort?
4. "The joy of the LORD is your strength," we read in Nehemiah 8:10 (NKJV). What are some of the ways the joy of the Lord strengthens you?
5. How is the growth of joy in your life similar to the ripening of fruit?
6. What is the difference between receiving joy and achieving joy? Which is easier for you? Which is better for you?

Chapter 9: The Narrow Path

1. Can you describe your unique path, designed by God just for you?
2. In what ways do you see God leading you on your narrow path?
3. What are some of the circumstances that have narrowed your path?
4. In Matthew 7:13–14, Jesus tells us that we can enter God's kingdom only through the narrow gate. He uses three images to describe the "gateway to life." What are they?
5. "Two are better than one, because they have a good return for their labor: If either of them falls down, one can help the other up." This passage from Ecclesiastes 4:9–12 (NIV)

concludes with "A threefold cord is not [easily] broken" (NKJV). What do you know about how a threefold cord is constructed? (Google it, if you don't know.) This is a strong image of an important relationship. Who makes up the threefold cord?

Chapter 10: Potholes on the Path

1. What is the difference between conviction and condemnation? Which do you tend to feel the most? How can you know when you are experiencing condemnation versus conviction?
2. Read Psalm 119:125. What does the psalmist pray for? Have you ever prayed that prayer?
3. Describe some times that the Holy Spirit has gently corrected you. Was it effective?
4. Describe some personality traits listed in Ephesians 4:32.
5. Our minds are a battleground. What is a good defense God has given us to fight battles in our minds? (Hint: read Psalm 149:6.)
6. Why should you choose to praise God instead of worry? Can we trust God with this struggle?
7. Recognizing potholes in our lives can help us avoid destruction. How can we improve in responding to the God-given warnings that protect us?

Chapter 11: The Path of God for You

1. List three to five of the things we can do to find and follow our God-ordained path.
2. Why is praise so powerful? How does it change us?
3. Describe your understanding of a partnership with God. Why

is the partnership important? How do we partner with God in His miracles today?

4. What does Jesus teach us about giving?

Thank you for walking this path with me!

Notes

Chapter 4: Prayers for the Path: Ask God

1. Craig von Buseck, "The Legacy of George Washington Carver," CBN, May 17, 2010, https://www1.cbn.com/ChurchWatch/archive/2010/05/17/the-legacy-of-george-washington-carver.

2. The Book of Common Prayer and Administration of the Sacraments and Other Rites and Ceremonies of the Church: Together with the Psalter or Psalms of David According to the Use of the Episcopal Church (New York: Church Publishing, 1979), 308.

Chapter 5: The Parenting Path: Getting Started

1. *The Edison and Ford Quote Book* (n.p.: Edison & Ford Winter Estates, 2004), 4.

Chapter 8: The Path of Joy

1. Billy James Foote, "You Are My King (Amazing Love)," 2003.

About the Author

Lisa Nelson Robertson is a noted author and teacher with more than thirty years' experience in leading women's Bible studies. Following a successful advertising and sales career in Boston, she and her husband, Tim, moved to Virginia Beach, Virginia, where she devoted herself to raising five children and was an active leader in women's ministries.

After her move to Virginia Beach, Lisa founded Changing Seasons, an outreach designed to help women discover and grow deeper in their faith. Hosted in prominent locations throughout the country, Changing Seasons has proudly welcomed popular speakers, including Korie Robertson, Lysa TerKeurst, Katherine and Jay Wolf, and Wimbledon champion Betsy McCormick.

Lisa is also an advocate for the importance of early childhood education, serving as a founding board member of E-3, Elevate Early Education, a statewide initiative in Virginia promoting school readiness for children under five. Lisa pioneered the implementation of Faithful Beginnings in low-income housing projects and was appointed by Virginia's governor in 2012 to serve on the Virginia State Board of Child Abuse and Neglect.

In addition to her outreach programs, Lisa has authored a series of Bible study guides and published an Advent guide, *Making*

Christmas About Christ, which also appears as an annual feature on *The 700 Club*.

Lisa earned a BA from Sweet Briar College and lives in Virginia with her husband. Their five children are grown, and she enjoys life with their expanding group of ten grandchildren.